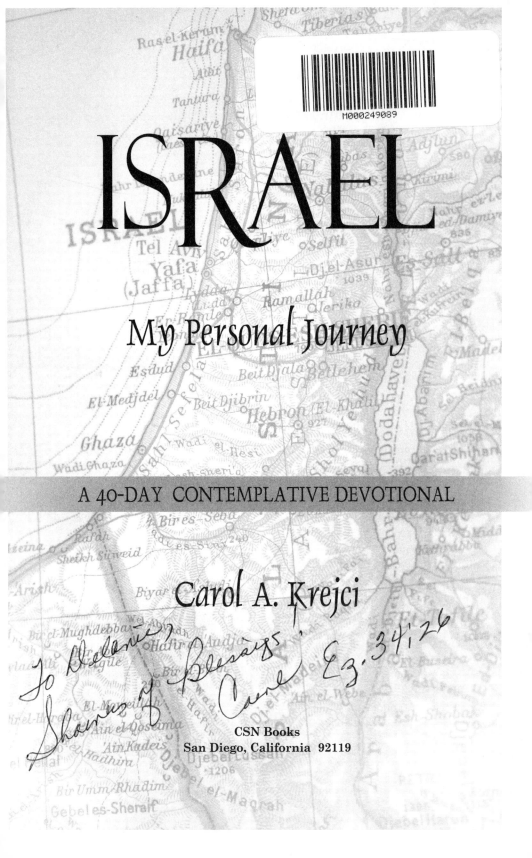

ISRAEL

My Personal Journey

A 40-DAY CONTEMPLATIVE DEVOTIONAL

Carol A. Krejci

CSN Books
San Diego, California 92119

ISRAEL, MY PERSONAL JOURNEY
Copyright © 2010 by Carol A. Krejci

ISBN: 978-1-59352-392-3

Published by:

CSN Books
7287 Birchcreek Rd.
San Diego, CA 92119
Toll-free: 1-866-757-9953

www.csnbooks.com

Scripture quotations marked NIV are taken from the NEW INTERNATIONAL VERSION, © 1973, 1978, and 1984, by the International Bible Society. Used by permission of Zondervan Publishing.

Scripture quotations marked NASB are taken from the NEW AMERICAN STANDARD BIBLE, © 1960, 1962, 1963, 1968, 1971, 1972, 1973, 1975, 1977, 1995 by The Lockman Foundation. Used by permission.

Scripture quotations marked TLB are taken from THE LIVING BIBLE, © 1971. Used by permission of Tyndale House Publishers, Inc., Wheaton, Illinois 60189. All rights reserved.

Scripture quotations marked NKJV are taken from the NEW KING JAMES VERSION, © 1982 by Thomas Nelson, Inc. Used by permission. All rights reserved.

Scripture quotations marked KJV are taken from the KING JAMES VERSION, used by permission.

Scripture quotations marked AMP are taken from THE AMPLIFIED BIBLE, © 1954, 1958, 1962, 1964, 1965, 1987 by The Lockman Foundation. All rights reserved.

Scripture quotations marked NLT are taken from the NEW LIVING TRANSLATION, © 1996, 2004 by Tyndale Charitable Trust. Used by permission of Tyndale House Publishers.

Scripture quotations marked TNIV are taken from TODAY'S NEW INTERNATIONAL VERSION, © 2001, 2005 by Biblica.

Printed in the United States of America.

ACKNOWLEDGMENTS

An acknowledgment made at the completion of writing a book is a means by which to thank those involved in bringing a writer's vision to fruition. I have many to thank.

God brought me from Lancaster, Ohio to San Diego, California as a result of my prayers to be in an environment conducive to my attempts to write. It was a challenge when my prayers were answered because it meant leaving my home of 35 years, my personal possessions, my family and friends and heading for an unknown future. Although I had lived in the same San Diego area before, never had I left everything and commenced on a journey with no knowledge of where I would live or how I would earn enough money to support my happy habit of living in San Diego and writing books.

The Lord provided abundantly for all of my needs, sometimes in the most amazing ways. He provided my friend Eithne Keegan, R.N. missionary, whom He sent to go alongside me from the moment He gave me the "go-ahead" to fulfill my dreams. Without her encouragement, I would have never attempted to come out of retirement as an R.N. and obtain a California nurse's license at my age. She spent countless hours on the phone helping me to complete what seemed like mountains of paperwork in order to accomplish this. She then flew east from her home in southern California, taking three weeks of her vacation time to accompany me on the westward journey. She encouraged me at every obstacle I saw as insurmountable and prayed with me and for me when I became fearful, homesick or doubting. With my car practically overflowing with clothes, suitcases, and everything in between, we traveled this beautiful land, visited with dear friends and relatives and even made new ones along the way. The trip is a book unto itself and perhaps one day, I shall write it. Thank you, Eithne, for your ever-present support and encouragement, for your belief in following the leading of the Lord, for being a prayer partner and earthly paraclete to one as needy as me.

When I arrived in California, the first thing I did was drop in at the office of Therese Yang, M.D., at which time she hired me as a part-time nurse, thus enabling me to earn a living and also to help care for Lyme Disease patients. I have grown to love and admire her as she ministers without reimbursement of any kind to her very special patients. With loving staff members and hugs all around, her patients receive the best that God has to offer. Prayer circles are not uncommon in her small medical office. Thank you, Dr. Yang, for accepting me into your sphere of loving health care and for telling your patients, "This is my nurse, Carol...God brought her out of retirement and sent her to me." Your words and hugs are often what sustained me when times were tiring and discouraging due to my Chronic Fatigue Syndrome.

My dear friend Julie Kirk, in the meantime, had found the perfect living spot for me, in a location I had specifically asked God for many years prior to the move. Within a week, my home was filled with beautiful furniture and everything I needed to be comfortable; all of it provided by the goodness of her friends and family. I needed to spend very little in order to "set up housekeeping."

Encouragement regarding my health, my writing and my homesickness came from many sources: my family, my friends in California and Ohio and my new-found international friends at Shepherd of Hope Christian Chat Room for Chronic Illness. Phone calls, emails, prayers and cards did much to reassure me that I was in the right place at the right time, for so often questions loomed large in my mind. Thank you to everyone who encouraged me along this path.

My gratitude knows no bounds regarding the publishing of this book. Without the faithful guidance and tender attention to details provided to me by Gary and Julie Kirk, CSN Books, I might have given up long ago. Persistent encouragement and belief in what *Israel, My Personal Journey* would offer others, along with our deep commitment to the Lord, were part and parcel of our business relationship. Julie's excellent proofing and editing skills, her perfectionism and love of the written word were exactly what I needed to continue on for these many months of writing and rewriting the manuscript. Gary's business acumen is being utilized to enable me to "expand my tent" and bring the book to more people than I ever thought possible. Thank you, Gary and Julie, for believing in the concept of this book and in my ability to write it.

With a humble heart, I thank my children and friends who allowed me to follow God's leading without guilt or fear. Their steadfast support of me during this time has been immeasurable and I will ever be grateful for their consistent support and unconditional love. You are all my precious treasures.

Thank you Mary "Shep" Wilson, founder of Shepherd of Hope (www.shepherdofhope.org) and to Pastor Harold Sturm for your friendship and willingness to read the manuscript before it was published. I am very grateful indeed for your input and comments offered before the publishing of the book. Thank you to my cousin Bill Dickerson for your insight and advice. My deepest love and gratitude is expressed to the members of the Lancaster, Ohio Christian Writer's Group for cultivating the seeds for this book that God had planted in my mind so long ago.

Most importantly, thank You Lord, for showing me new vistas, for allowing me to see the land of the Bible and for urging me on to write this book. I pray it pleases You and brings the readers to a deeper understanding of how wonderful You are and how very much You love them.

TABLE OF CONTENTS

FOREWORD

Carol and I were introduced to each other at McDonald's for lunch one day through her granddaughter and my son. She asked me what I did for a living, I told her I was a publisher, she just so "happened" to have her first manuscript with her, and that was the beginning of our beautiful relationship. That manuscript, by the way, birthed in 2005, was Carol's first book entitled *Sowin' Seeds and Touchin' Lives*, a loving tribute to her dear friend Stephanie Whitcraft.

Carol is the definition of a true friend—one who is a gifted listener, whose compassion knows no end and considers her friends more important than herself. I have witnessed Carol's personal losses, her physical ailments and the way she has handled grief, and these experiences have only added to the insight and wisdom interwoven in this inspiring book you are about to read. Many of her friends join me when I say I will be eternally grateful to my heavenly Father for allowing me the privilege of knowing her in this lifetime.

Israel, My Personal Journey is designed to be a 40-day devotional as well as a personal tour for the reader seen through Carol's eyes as she lived her lifelong dream to visit the Holy Land in 1988, the 40th anniversary of Israel's statehood. It begins with the traveler's arrival in modern-day Israel and poignantly ends with the last days leading up to Christ's resurrection.

You will witness Abraham's painful choice to sacrifice his only son as you contemplate Father God's choice to offer His only Son, the unblemished Lamb of God who was given for us. Witness Jesus sentenced to death, join the denizens of Jerusalem as they speculate, dispute and question the occurrence of the resurrection, and understand the Seven Feasts (the obligatory feasts).

Visit a remnant of the Western Wall—holiest site of the Jewish faith, witness the Holocaust Memorial, see the place of the Dead

Sea Scrolls, and learn about the crudely-carved block of stone in Megiddo. As you enter into Jerusalem during the last week of Jesus' life, you will be challenged to experience the hidden mysteries of the Old Testament Feasts and their connection with Jesus' life and death.

Aided by her copious notes, detailed journal writing and attention to detail, Carol's in-depth research on the history and geography of Israel lays a strong foundational backdrop for this insightful travelogue. Her deep grasp of Old Testament scriptures is evident and Carol's rich spiritual applications will surely challenge and convict you.

You are about to embark on a journey of a lifetime. Through the pages of these devotionals, may the power of the Holy Spirit touch your life, increase your faith and deepen your intimacy with Him— it certainly has mine—as you join Carol in this extraordinary pilgrimage through Israel.

Julie Kirk
Vice President
CSN Books

INTRODUCTION

*Ask the LORD your God for a sign, whether in
the deepest depths or in the highest heights.*

Isaiah 7:11, NIV

When I visited the Holy Land in 1988, I did not expect to be writing a book about the trip these many years later. However, I did write in my journal as faithfully as possible, for I desired to always remember the sights and sounds of this wondrous place.

Who among us has not said at one time or another, "Oh, to walk where Jesus walked, Lord, would be my desire." Yes, to visit the land of the Bible and see the actual places we have heard of all our lives would be the thrill of a lifetime and although it had always been my deepest desire, I never expected my wish to become a reality. God had other plans for me, however, and as I slowly acknowledged that indeed it was His desire for me to visit the land, He planned every step of the way without flaw.

International Hospital Christian Fellowship (IHCF), an organization devoted to enabling medical workers to share their faith with their patients and co-workers, was planning a conference in Jerusalem for May of 1988. Although I had been an active member of the USA HCF for a number of years, I was astonished when I received an invitation to attend this conference, the chosen theme being "Endtime Overcomers." HCF members representing at least 90 countries would be attending. IHCF's founder, Frances Grimm, along with Brother Andrew, International HCF Promoter, author of the book *God's Smuggler* and founder of *Open Doors Ministry*, were the keynote speakers. I was thrilled to have even been considered as a potential attendee. My immediate thought, however, was simply a firm negative. There is no way I can attend this conference, I thought.

As a young girl, I had always longed to see the Holy City and as my Aunt Jeanie and I would sing the beautiful song of the same name, I would drift off into my own reverie, seeing myself in a place that now only my imagination could describe. I often told the Lord I would be forever content if only I could see Jerusalem. I knew I was not alone in this, for so many of us have had the same desire to see the land of the Bible. This was simply a wish, a hope, but I really never expected Him to grant me this privilege. In retrospect, however, I recognize that I had never asked Him for the opportunity either. The Bible tells us that we have not because we have not asked (John 16:24).

In the spring of 1988, the opportunity to go to the Holy Land had arisen and yet I felt I couldn't act on the invitation due to lack of finances, other commitments and the waning energy I was experiencing as a result of Chronic Fatigue Syndrome. This group of symptoms included indescribable exhaustion, aching joints and muscles, difficulty concentrating and most of all, a sleep disorder that interrupted my nighttime rest by awakening me every hour on the hour, or so it seemed. In the natural, I had every excuse not to go to the Holy Land and yet the Lord showed me that excuses are not valid when He has set His hand upon your life and has a plan for you. What we need to do is hear from Him, trust Him and act upon His direction with full confidence that the Great Creator will not send us off on some poorly planned journey. I had simply assumed the trip was out of the question. This thought was shattered a few weeks later when a thought penetrated my mind which would not let go. It was simply this:

"Don't you *want* to be an 'Endtime Overcomer,' Carol?"

I cautiously wondered, is this from God? Is He really speaking to me about this trip? Soon I found myself responding to the repeated question, "Oh yes, Lord, I *do* want to be an 'overcomer.' I will go, if you will just make a way for me."

That day, I had no more courage, stamina or money than I'd had the day I received the invitation, but God had provided the impetus I needed by placing a question in my mind. He also provided me with the boldness to proceed.

My decision to move forward came after much prayer and the Lord provided the confirmation I asked for through His Word, by agreement with fellow Christians and most especially by the peace that settled within my spirit. I knew that it was the direction He had chosen for me.

Though it was rather late to send in an application, I filled out the form and sent it (ten days late) to IHCF headquarters in South Africa, believing God would make a way. It was received at the office, processed and accepted in an amazingly short period of time, for I received the acceptance letter just 13 days later! Applying for a passport, something I had never done before, proceeded with lightning speed. I was advised by friends to go to the local post office for a passport application, but the gentleman I spoke with there suggested I go "around the corner" to our Congressman's office. "Perhaps he can facilitate the process," the postal worker suggested. With mounting excitement, I walked down the main steps of the post office and directly to the Congressman's office just a few buildings away! The receptionist listened to my request, placed a passport application into her typewriter and proceeded to ask the necessary questions of me. Within 15 minutes, she was finished and assured me that the application would be in the mail to Washington, D.C. that very day. She mentioned that because it was coming from the Congressman's office, it would not be placed at the end of the many requests (since they are always filed in order of their arrival), but instead would receive priority attention! The passport arrived in my mailbox in record time, I am told (in 11 days instead of the usual six weeks) on April 4th, the same day I received my acceptance letter from IHCF! God is a wonderful travel agent!!

At the time that I received the invitation, I was operating a small gift shop and although it was rewarding in many ways, I was losing money every day. After months of trying to succeed, I finally decided to sell the inventory at a greatly reduced price, close the shop and return to a more substantial means of earning money...nursing.

Only recently, while writing this book, did I come across a small notation in my Bible reflective of my role in making this trip. God covered the cost of the airfare and the souvenir money in quite unexpected ways. Apparently, I used my savings to pay for the cost of the conference and other pre-trip incidentals as this quote from my journal will attest:

May 10, 1988 – "...going to Jerusalem tomorrow—must give up my bank account to get there. God tests me about money—sent a double rainbow last night."

A newly-diagnosed health problem, Chronic Fatigue Syndrome, had adversely affected my stamina, so I opted for a part-time job, which of course meant diminished earning power. I knew I physically could not work more than three days a week. Little did I know, however, that when my taxes for the year were prepared, the financial reverses related to the shop would provide me with a tax rebate check equivalent to the cost of the airfare to Israel! Thus, the loss actually reversed itself and became a gain.

I became more excited as God continued to reveal to me that this trip was indeed part of His plan for me. I had no fear of traveling alone halfway around the world, despite family and friends' dire warnings and deep concerns regarding the political situation in the Middle East. I earnestly began to study more about the country in preparation for the journey. With new boldness, I was able to ask the Lord for "just a few hundred dollars" for souvenirs for my family and friends. Since I had no extra funds, He graciously and astoundingly provided the amount I asked for. He did this so rapidly (over a weekend!), that to this day, I am amazed at the way this amount of money materialized in such a very short period of time. God was in the recycling business long before it was fashionable and in this instance, it was money!

Did He want me to go to the Holy Land? Yes, I know that He did and I would like to share with you some amazing insights I gathered along the way. The Lord is always teaching us and showing us ways to share the blessings of walking along our life's way with Him. I am excited to be able to share some pictures in story form He provided me while on my journey as a pilgrim to this wondrous place of the Bible. I pray you will enjoy this little excursion and be blessed just as I was to see something new and exciting from the land of God. His parables do not require much imagination, for they are simply the telling of tales from an earthly and everyday point of view. However, parables are also used by the Lord as a means of teaching us spiritual comparisons. In this case, I will be sharing some of what I feel God revealed to me as I traveled the Holy Land for ten days. I hope you enjoy the trip!

If you believe, you will receive
whatever you ask for in prayer.

Matthew 21:22, NIV

PREFACE

The stony silent computer seemed to be beckoning me that chilly Ohio March morning. I absently muttered in reply, "Later, OK? I have too many other things I'd like to do right now. First of all, it is time for my coffee and devotions. I want to see what God is saying to me and go from there."

However, I didn't get much further along in my plans for the day. Contemplating the message in the devotional regarding listening to God, I asked, "Lord, do You *really* want me to tell Your stories? I have doubts regarding my abilities, yet You have shown me kindness and grace regarding my writing. Your direction has consistently been so clear to me. I know what I want to write next...in fact, much of it was written many years ago and it remains a strong force within me today. Do I dare begin another book? Please, talk to me."

I walked to the computer and a thought permeated my mind. "The printer has not been used for several months...connect it now," I thought. I gathered the cables and wires necessary and connected them all a bit fearfully. To my surprise, it worked! Did I think for a minute that it wouldn't?

My dear friend (also editor and proofreader) Julie had advised me when I started writing my first book, *Sowin' Seeds and Touchin' Lives* that the first step to a book's reality is to create a Title Page. "After that," she said, "add a Table of Contents...this will cause it to become real to you."

I hesitantly sat down and created a "new document" in the word processor and titled it *Israel*. It was almost noon by the time I finally stopped typing. I had, on what had just hours before been an empty desk in front of me, not only a Title Page, but also a Table of Contents and a completed Introduction...the book had been birthed!

Actually, God had been talking to me all along regarding this little book about Israel. When I toured the country with IHCF in 1988, I came away with what I saw as some unique interpretations regarding some of the sights I beheld. Analogies with applications, I had thought. Shortly after returning from Israel, I taught a Sunday school class on this topic and the outlines and information for some of the classes now comprise the basis for this book.

God's story is not new, but the presentation often is because the reading and listening audience is so diverse. Perhaps these particular insights given to me were just for you, the reader. If so, I pray you will enjoy this trip, placed in the setting of a tour and described by myself. We will begin with a short history of the land, an arrival by plane and then a brief, but rough and rugged taxi ride to the Holy City—Jerusalem! Come along!

1. THE LAND

Go, assemble the elders of Israel and say to them,
"The LORD, the God of your fathers—the God
of Abraham, Isaac and Jacob—appeared to
me and said: 'I have watched over you and
have seen what has been done to you in Egypt.
And I have promised to bring you up out of
your misery in Egypt into the land of the
Canaanites, Hittites, Amorites, Perizzites,
Hivites and Jebusites—a land flowing
with milk and honey.'"

Exodus 3:16-17, NIV

After 400 years of oppression in Egypt, God brought to His people a man of His own choosing to lead them out of their cruel circumstances. The man Moses, born a Jew, raised by the Pharaoh's daughter and eventually expelled from his position of favor, met with the God of the Hebrews 40 years later while tending his father-in-law Jethro's flocks at the edge of the desert near Horeb, the mountain of God. After his conversation with God, Moses met with the elders, told them of his encounter and explained that God had designated him (Moses) to lead the people out of Egyptian captivity.

Moses and Aaron brought together all the elders of
the Israelites, and Aaron told them everything the
LORD had said to Moses. He also performed the
signs before the people, and they believed. And
when they heard that the LORD was concerned
about them and had seen their misery, they
bowed down and worshiped.

Exodus 4:29-31, NIV

Exodus 12 tells of God's specific instructions for the observance of the first-ever Passover. It is amazing to me that on the night *before* the exodus began, they were told by the Lord to enter into a remembrance of His soon-to-be-performed miracle—their release from slavery. This night *before* they left the land of Egypt was when they had to sacrifice the lamb and place its blood upon their doorposts. I'm sure that required a lot of faith in a great God, for until this time, Pharaoh had not been intimidated by the many plagues God had sent. What bolstered their faith on this night of all nights?

The Lord also told them to eat in haste the lamb, bitter herbs and unleavened bread, but that they were to do this in their traveling clothes. Imagine that! What an act of faith it was to perform this unknown ritual in the blackness of a fear-filled night! Had they not obeyed His directive, the result would have been the deaths of their own first-born sons.

There is a great lesson here for us...when all else seems bleak and hopeless in our lives, when we feel ensnared by our circumstances whatever they may be, we need to remember to celebrate God's deliverance *before* it even takes place. He will perform His miraculous deliverance in His perfect way and in His perfect timing, just as He promised! It is *definitely* a matter of faith!

By faith (simple trust and confidence in God) he [Moses]
*instituted and carried out the Passover and the sprinkling
of the blood [on the doorposts], so that the destroyer of the
first-born (the angel) might not touch those
[of the children of Israel].*

Hebrews 11:28, AMP

2. MARCHING ON

Then the Lord said to Moses, "Quit praying
and get the people moving! Forward, march!"

Exodus 14:15, TLB

That night, the Israelites began their long sojourn to the Promised Land. Free at last from the misery of Egyptian domination, they celebrated with much thanksgiving. According to the Bible, a massive number of people and animals embarked on a journey to freedom. Exodus 12:37 says there were about six hundred thousand men on foot, plus all of the women and children; many other people also left with them, as well as great numbers of livestock, both flocks and herds.

It wasn't long before this happiness and gratitude turned to grumbling and complaining. As we read the story of the exodus, we see time and again the waxing and waning of the Israelites' faith in God as their provider. Their happiness would be replaced by a pattern of cries of distress followed by God's rescue and the subsequent rejoicing of the Hebrews. As they traveled through the desert, there was much complaining about the lack of meat and other foods familiar to them in Egypt, so God supplied quail and manna. When they needed water, the Lord provided it, when their feet got tired, He kept their walking shoes in such condition that they never wore out, and when they violated their covenant agreement with the golden calf, Moses interceded for them.

After 40 long years of wandering, they reached the Promised Land, conquered it and eventually became a nation of people loyal to Jehovah, the one true God. He bountifully blessed them in this new land and in gratitude, sacrifices and offerings to the Lord were made. Thousands of years later, there would come another who would make the ultimate sacrifice. Yes, many years later Israel's Savior was heralded by the angels of Heaven—only this time, the nation of Israel represented *all* of mankind and when God became the man Jesus, the atonement for the sins of *all* people was covered forevermore.

Israel

Israel is located on the continent of Asia in the central part of the Middle East. About the size of New Jersey, with an area of 8,000 square miles, Israel is bordered by four states: to the north, Lebanon; northeast, Syria; east, Jordan; southwest, Egypt. To the west, it lies on the smooth eastern shore of the Mediterranean Sea; from there, chalk plains lead eastward to limestone hills, which drop steeply through the eroded Wilderness of Judea to the Jordan Valley. In the north, Mount Hermon is where the Jordan River begins and then empties into Lake Hula dropping rapidly (900 feet in ten miles) into the Sea of Galilee. From there, it winds through the Jordan Valley, eventually reaching 1,292 feet below sea level at the Dead Sea, a body of water with no outlet, filled with bromide and salt. The seasons in Israel vary from the extreme heat in summer (May to August) with its hot, dry desert winds to cool, wet winter days (November through April) when snow can be seen on the mountains. Galilee is known to be the coldest and wettest region during the winter.

Jerusalem

A 1580 map of the Middle Ages clearly showed Israel, with Europe, Asia and Africa bordering, to be the center of the world, while its capital Jerusalem was placed at the center of Israel. In this rather artistic and symbolic depiction, Jerusalem was actually seen as the center of the known world at the time of the crusades not so many centuries ago! Eventually, as cartographers were provided with more accurate instruments with which to measure distance, etc., the maps became more and more realistic.

Jerusalem was already over 2,000 years old when King David captured it from the Jebusites and renamed it the City of David.

Located 33 miles inland from the Mediterranean Sea, Jerusalem sits in the Judean highlands at the edge of the wilderness. It stands on a curved ridge formed by two valleys, the Kidron Valley to the east and Hinnom Valley to the west. The Bible tells us that Abraham, who was born around 2165 BC, received bread and wine from the city's king, Melchizedek.

> *Then Melchizedek king of Salem brought out bread and wine. He was priest of God Most High, and he blessed Abram, saying, "Blessed be Abram by God Most High, Creator of heaven and earth."*

Genesis 14:18-19, NIV

Chronicles regarding Jerusalem's blazing history of repeated settlements and conquests reach into antiquity. Over the millennia, it has been conquered by Egyptians, Jebusites, Israelites, Babylonians (586 BC), Persians (538 BC), Greeks, Romans (63 BC), Arabs (683 AD), crusaders (1099 AD), Mamelukes (1260 AD) and Ottomans (1517-1917 AD).

Today, there remains strife and threats of war in this land of the Bible, yet we know that God has set apart this region of the world for His purposes. It is my hope that as you read this book, you will not let a day go by without praying for Israel and the peace of Jerusalem. One day soon, there will be no more war, no more tears or sorrow and we will behold the Lamb of God once more in all His glory.

Behold the Lamb!

John 1:29, NASB

3. TROOPS ON THE TARMAC

"The word of the LORD you have spoken is good,"
Hezekiah replied. For he thought, "Will there
not be peace and security in my lifetime?"

2 Kings 20:19, NIV

In a gentle, slow descent, we glided earthward. As our jumbo jet prepared for a landing, the view from the window provided the perfect presentation for arriving in the Holy Land, for from my window blue expanses mirrored each other—above, a clear, azure sky and below, a glistening, sapphire Mediterranean Sea! What a welcome to the land where the blue Star of David would be flying from every flagpole and window—I was totally entranced with the thought! Sooner than I expected, the plane's landing gear was released and an easy touchdown in Israel, the Holy Land of God, quickly followed.

We had arrived in Tel Aviv, capital of Israel, which this year was celebrating the 40th anniversary of its statehood. My anticipation for what lay ahead could scarcely be contained! Jerusalem was now only 30 miles away! Disbelief at this reality accompanied me as I exited the plane. I was a bit surprised that the plane did not taxi to the gate, but rather, parked on the tarmac, necessitating a gingerly-stepped walk down the jumbo jet's clanking metal stairway. My first steps in Israel therefore occurred as my feet touched down on what I thought of as holy ground—namely, a tarmac.

The culture shock was immediate, for stepping off the plane brought me face-to-face with soldiers, guns and other evidence that the citizens of this land paid very close attention to security and the possibility of war. Not surprisingly, this military presence gave me an immediate, but fleeting sense of *insecurity*! Neither our travel itinerary nor my gentle life in America had prepared me for this!

As I write this today in 2010, sadly, we in America also must taste the bitter pill of terrorism and its inevitable consequences. Precautionary measures such as finger-printing, security checks, identity protection and "terrorism levels" being announced frequently over public address systems at all of our airports have become the norm in America. We must now acknowledge that our great land sits in the midst of a fragile and potentially explosive worldwide setting, one that yields distrust, fear and anxiety. We in America remain novices and perhaps more than a little naive in matters of national defense.

Israel was quite advanced in 1988 regarding security issues and ten days later, as I prepared to leave Israel, I was equally impressed to learn that it was even more difficult to leave the country than it was to enter it. At the same airport in Tel Aviv, we were required to arrive three hours in advance of our flight, endure penetrating questions as to our purpose for being in Israel and have our luggage *thoroughly* inspected by security personnel. I was asked if anyone had presented me with gifts or had given me a package to deliver to another person. I was also queried as to why I was wearing a Star of David necklace, a souvenir I had bought in downtown Jerusalem. The man checking my luggage went so far as to ask me why I, who claimed to be a Christian, was wearing a piece of jewelry that represented the state of Israel. I never thought of this as anything but wisdom and never for a moment did I feel that I was being profiled—the screening method was the same for everyone. Trying as it was at times, I found the process to be unmistakably comforting even though it was extremely time-consuming and so very early in the morning. When it was finally time to board the plane, I felt safer than I had ever felt before. Security is a good practice indeed!

Spiritually speaking, there is but one security worth having and that is the security of knowing you are safe in the palm of God's hand, hidden beneath His wing and waiting for your eternal reward, which is to be with Him forever in Heaven. The following words of Jesus, which are so often quoted, sum it up perfectly—may we always be encouraged and hide them in our hearts and minds, not only during our earthly journeys, but during our spiritual ones as well.

> *I have told you these things, so that in me you may*
> *have peace. In this world you will have trouble.*
> *But take heart! I have overcome the world.*

John 16:33, NIV

4. BEYOND THE GATE

I will bring them back to live in Jerusalem; they
will be my people, and I will be faithful and
righteous to them as their God.

Zechariah 8:8, NIV

A sense of excitement and wonderment filled my heart and mind as I stepped outside the Tel Aviv Ben Gurion International Airport terminal. I am actually here in God's Holy Land! I cannot believe it is true! I am incredulous! I thought.

It was not too crowded within the building, but outside it became a different world. I saw hundreds of Jewish people behind a tall, black iron gate and as we walked by, I realized that they were all awaiting the arrival of their family members or friends. "Perhaps they haven't seen each other for twenty or more years," I was told by the person who was accompanying me.

There was such jubilance and anticipation in the air! Some of the people were in contemporary dress, but many of the men were in the traditional Orthodox garb, wearing white shirts beneath the buttoned jacket of their black suits and the accustomed black fedora hat atop their heads. Each man had a beard and the curly side-locks in front of his ears.

I thought I was stepping into history for it was indeed the final days of the Diaspora. Jews were returning to their homeland after more than 2,000 years of being scattered all over the world and under such persecution that there should be no one left. Yet, this year, 1988, they were celebrating the 40th anniversary of the statehood of their reclaimed land of Israel!

There was much hustle and bustle beyond the gate. Voices were raised in eager anticipation of seeing and holding loved ones once again after so many years. Perhaps for the majority, the thought of such a reunion had seemed impossible until today. Great numbers of Jews were emigrating from communist lands; some perhaps had even been prisoners. Later, in another chapter, I will tell you about a Russian Christian who had been imprisoned and then set free! It is an exciting example of the importance of commitment to prayer.

But for now, let us return to the reunion beyond the gate. As people exited the terminal and entered into the bright sunlight, those who had been waiting were jumping up and down excitedly calling out to their loved ones. It was a sight to behold! Together again! Praise to the Almighty One!

As an observer, my prayer to God was that Jesus would return soon, so that we all might be joined together in that heavenly place beyond the gate. "But wait, dear Lord," I pleaded, "not until all of my children are saved, for I want to be reunited with all four of them in eternity!" God reminded me ever-so-gently that He is not willing that *any* of His children be left behind and when the great reunion time arrives, His heart's desire is that they *all* be there.

I found myself thinking back to the time when my four children were all together at my home some months before. It was the first such reunion in many years and they were so happy to be together that despite my having adequate bed space, they chose not to go to bed. At 2 a.m. I found the four of them sprawled about the living room floor—they just wanted to be near each other.

The Lord told me to pay attention to my deep joy in seeing them all together at last, after all the trials, difficulties and losses they each had endured. I remembered the deep satisfaction I had felt seeing them there under my roof and realized that the Lord desires the same for His precious family.

"What can I do, Lord, to make this possible, for I desire your return. This world is such a mess!"

"Go and be my witness," He seemed to say, *"and when the going gets rough, remember the scene on the living room floor. You are simply helping me."*

It is truly a privilege to be a part of God's marvelous plan of salvation. He already knows how, when, where and with whom our special encounters will occur, and together we will tell the world that God is love and He is eagerly awaiting our arrival at the gate. Let us strive to bring those we meet on our life's journey along with us.

He will wipe every tear from their eyes, and there will be
no more death or sorrow or crying or pain.
All these things are gone forever.

Revelation 21:4, NLT

31

5. WILD RIDE TO JERUSALEM

God's reputation is very great in Judah and
in Israel. His home is in Jerusalem.
He lives upon Mt. Zion.

Psalm 76:1-2, TLB

In those brief moments outside the Ben Gurion International Airport, I was mentally transported to an ancient world I had only dreamed of, but the wild, 35-minute ride to Jerusalem (provided by an adventurous, risk-taking taxi driver), very quickly brought me back to reality. Indeed, the entire trip would continue to bounce me back and forth between the old and the new.

A similar experience will be yours as you travel along. Be prepared for this dichotomy, for ancient cities and towns have frequently been modernized or made marketable, while others lie in ruins—desolate spots with their memories buried beneath layers upon layers of time and rubble. Often this fact can render one disappointed and sad or give a deep sense of disillusionment. Harsher still is the reality that although you are visiting the Holy Land and its sacred places, these same sites are most likely simply traditional locations and are not authentic. Although many cities and towns are still in their original geographic locations, thousands of years, multitudes of wars and their ensuing cultural changes have occurred. Much will not be as it has appeared in your mind's eye.

Anticipation grew within my heart as we endured the somewhat frightening 34-mile ride to Jerusalem. With wheels screeching and dust flying in our wake, the driver deftly skimmed the dirt borders of the paved and winding road leading to the Holy City. This was no time to feel poetic. We were holding onto our seats and handgrips for dear life, barely able to take in the view. Somehow, I managed to scratch a few notes in my journal:

> "The land is flat to rolling with orange groves and hay bales dotting the dry earthen landscape—so reminiscent of non-irrigated areas of southern California; brown, arid land sparsely populated with native trees and shrubs."

We were pilgrims following the ancient way of millions who have preceded us and it was indeed incredulous!

The Holy City, long a place of dreams and imagination, was about to enter my field of vision. My heart was racing along with the taxicab on a road I sensed was leading me home. It was an inexplicable sense of nearness to God and totally unexpected. My eyes strained, reaching for our destination. Soon, there was a glimpse of gold in the distance and quickly, the city of Jerusalem was seen, seemingly nestled within the cradle of the dry, distant hills close to the horizon. Home at last, I thought...thank You, dear Lord, for granting me this privilege.

As you enter into this place, remember that just as the Bible continually speaks to each of us, so will Jerusalem; so will the land. Listen as you travel and it will talk to you, not so much by way of the sites you will visit, but by the faith that brings you here...faith in your loving Creator Father, who chose to leave His Heavenly abode and come to earth to be born, live and die in human form, to pave the way and pay the cost for our salvation.

Jerusalem

Ancient city, place of God,
Where the suffering feet of our Savior have trod,
As I enter your City of Peace on the hill,
Speak to me, Father, show me your will.

*You are the light of the world. A city on
a hill cannot be hidden.*

Matthew 5:14, NIV

6. JERUSALEM, STILL STANDING!

Those who trust in the LORD are like Mount Zion,
which cannot be shaken but endures forever.

Psalm 125:1, NIV

The closer we approached to Jerusalem, the higher it appeared to be, for it is built upon a mountain ridge more than 2,500 feet above sea level. The city that had appeared from a distance to be snuggled amongst the hills now encompassed my entire field of vision. Surrounded by mountains as it had for ages, it beckoned to my spirit and spoke to me of eternity.

As the mountains surround Jerusalem,
so the LORD surrounds his people
both now and forevermore.

Psalm 125:2, NIV

God's Holy City remains despite having been destroyed fourteen times; its ancient stone walls are pockmarked with evidence of the battles it has endured, yet is still standing! My eyes glistened with tears, adding sparkle to the vision before me.

Over 3,000 years old, Jerusalem is a city of winding, narrow, paved streets and modern, busy car-filled roadways, distinctly containing the old and the new. On the first part of our tour, we will visit the new; at the end of our journey, we shall visit the old.

Modern buildings, condominiums, universities, hospitals and museums are among the structures of modern Jerusalem. It is indeed a culture shock to see the Jerusalem of today, but City of God it is and so it shall remain. Amazingly (and I think we all know this), it is the center of not one, but three world faiths; Jewish, Christian and Muslim and as it has been for thousands of years, so it remains—the place where so many go to meet with God.

Contemporary architecture defines the Knesset, the location of the seat of the Israeli government today. It is indeed amazing that not so many years ago, Jews by the millions were perishing, not only within the concentration camps of Germany, but everywhere the relentless Nazis searched them out. (A visit to Yad Vashem later this week will open this horrible page of world history to us in a form of unspeakable reality.)

What deeply touched my spirit then and still does is the fact that despite its multi-millennial history of battles and bloodshed, it stands today where it has always stood—built on solid rock in the highlands of Judea! Although the glorious Temple is no longer there, I take comfort in the knowledge that we, the Church, are now the Temple of God and the dwelling place of His Holy Spirit.

Do you not know that your body is a temple of the Holy Spirit, who is in you, whom you have received from God? You are not your own.

1 Corinthians 6:19, NIV

We must consider this: Do we stand on that same solid rock of faith? This place where God said He would come down from Heaven to live among His people remains a visual assurance that God is keeping His Word to preserve it until Jesus returns and triumphantly enters the Golden Gates.

He is like a man which built an house, and digged deep, and laid the foundation on a rock: and when the flood arose, the stream beat vehemently upon that house, and could not shake it: for it was founded upon a rock.

Luke 6:48, KJV

7. THE TABERNACLE, THE TEMPLE AND ME

Then have them make a sanctuary for me,
and I will dwell among them.

Exodus 25:8, NIV

Before Moses' time, men devised their own means of giving thanks to God for His goodness to them. When Adam and Eve sinned in the Garden, they strung fig leaves to be used as clothing to hide their disobedience and sin. However, after God had pronounced their punishment, He covered them with garments made of the skins of animals. Thus, we see that with man's first sin, God required and also provided a blood covering.

The Lord God made garments of skin for
Adam and his wife and clothed them.

Genesis 3:21, NIV

Let's consider Cain and Abel's offerings of meat and grain, one of which was unacceptable to God. Have you ever wondered why Cain's offering was not acceptable to God? Bible experts state that there is no evidence of God having commanded specific offerings or sacrifices during that time. Could it be that even then God was looking within the heart of man?

Noah, after the flood, erected an altar and offered animal sacrifices to God.

Then Noah built an altar to the LORD and, taking
some of all the clean animals and clean birds, he
sacrificed burnt offerings on it.

Genesis 8:20, NIV

37

There are many instances recorded in the Bible that tell us about the patriarchs' building of earthen or stone altars and pillars in order to express their gratitude to Jehovah for His goodness to them. Wherever they went and settled, altars were also erected and on occasion even certain trees and wells were designated as sacred.

Years later, during their sojourn in the wilderness, after Moses returned from his mountain meeting with God, the Hebrews learned that not only had the Lord rendered the Ten Commandments, but He had also given Moses the plan for an altar housed in a tent as well (Exodus, chapters 25-27). With Moses as the mediator, God would come down among His people and meet with Moses in the tent. Although Moses wasn't actually a priest, when God spoke with him there, a cloudy pillar stood at the entrance signifying God's presence.

Various types of sacrifices were offered by the Levites who had been specified as priests by God. These were cereal, peace, sin and trespass offerings (money), along with burnt sacrifices. The main obligatory feasts held were the Sabbath, Passover, Pentecost, the Feast of the Tabernacles and lastly, the Day of Atonement. This was a day of fasting and repentance, when the sins of the people were transferred to a goat (scapegoat) who was then sent away from the camp to wander in the desert to die.

Jesus would one day give His life as the ultimate, perfect sacrifice for our sins and even His death upon the cross revealed the mystery of this ancient ritual. Just as the goat, upon whom all the sins of the people were placed, was sent out from the camp, so Jesus, carrying the sins of mankind, suffered and died outside the walls of the city (camp) that He loved so much—Jerusalem.

After David claimed Jerusalem as the capital of the nation, he believed that God should dwell in a place better than a tent. He bought the site (2 Samuel 24:18-25), but the Lord did not allow him to build the Temple. Some years later, his son Solomon supervised the building of the glorious Temple in Jerusalem. The celebration that took place when Solomon dedicated the Temple and brought the Ark of the Covenant from the portable Tabernacle to its new place of honor is found in 1 Kings, chapter 8.

In 586 BC, when the people were taken captive to Babylonia, the Temple was destroyed and the Ark of the Covenant was lost. Later, a remnant of people returned to rebuild it and following Moses' plan, a new Temple was built although it was smaller and less ornate.

The center of all Jewish worship was the Temple, but during the exile when Jews couldn't get to the Temple, local synagogues were instituted. There the Law of Moses and the law of the prophets were read and prayers were recited.

For Moses has been preached in every city from the earliest times and is read in the synagogues on every Sabbath.

Acts 15:21, NIV

According to our tour guide, all synagogues in Israel face Jerusalem where the Temple was, while those outside of Israel face east. I recall an Orthodox Jewish man in the huge Charles de Galle Airport in Paris who was praying and facing east...it was fascinating to me, especially since I was en route to Israel, but at the time, I did not understand the significance.

During the New Testament era, Herod the Great built a third Temple in an effort to assuage the unrest caused by Roman rule, but it was not totally finished until about 60 AD. However, Jerusalem fell to the Romans in 70 AD and once again, the Temple was destroyed, demonstrating Jesus' statement that not one stone of the Temple would remain unturned. Jesus loved and attended the Temple, but the time was coming when all people would worship God in spirit and in truth.

"Yet a time is coming and has now come when the true worshipers will worship the Father in spirit and truth, for they are the kind of worshipers the Father seeks."

John 4:23, NIV

The Temple was destroyed and never rebuilt. What remains yet today is the Western Wall, part of the wall Herod built to support the great platform of the Temple compound.

The old Tabernacle was but a shadow of the true ideal which is in Heaven. Jesus is our High Priest and He offered His own blood to ensure our eternal salvation, for without the shedding of blood there is no forgiveness of sin (Hebrews 9:22). God said He would write His laws into our hearts and minds and will remember our sins no more (Hebrews 10:16). How thankful we can be! We are the Temple now and for us, the Temple is not built of stone, but of the souls of the redeemed.

Don't you know that you yourselves are God's Temple and that God's Spirit lives in you? If anyone destroys God's Temple, God will destroy him; for God's Temple is sacred, and you are that Temple.

1 Corinthians 3:16-17, NIV

8. THE WESTERN WALL

Solomon made an alliance with Pharaoh king of Egypt and married his daughter. He brought her to the City of David until he finished building his palace and the temple of the LORD, and the wall around Jerusalem.

1 Kings 3:1, NIV

When we toured the modern city of Jerusalem, we began by visiting the holiest site of the Jewish faith—a remnant of the Western Wall built by Herod in 20 BC, and destroyed along with Jerusalem in 70 AD by the Romans. The Wall is located in a huge paved space closely guarded by Israeli soldiers who thoroughly inspected our purses before we were permitted to enter the area. The gold-gleaming Dome of the Rock, built in 685 AD by Islamic conquerors, was within view and the call to prayer could be heard all over.

Skull-capped men were to the left of a divider, while little girls, grandmas and mommas stood to the right, all praying and often crying with prayer books in hand. Leaning toward the ancient stone wall, praying men rapidly bent at the waist and then slowly assumed an upright position, bowing back and forth repetitively. We were told by our guide that the forward movement represents the haste to attend Temple and the slow resumption of the upright position represents one's reluctance to leave the Temple. For years Jews have cried at the Wall for the "glory of the past and misery of the present."

I was particularly interested in the partition (mechitza) between men and women and quickly learned from others that the dividing screen is there in keeping with Orthodox

Jewish tradition which does not allow women in the men's section. I soon found myself to the right of the mechitza, saying my prayers for all mankind and asking God to bring peace on earth. Tufts of grass peeked out from the crevices between the immense blocks of stone above my head, while closer to me, stuffed in every available space, were pieces of paper—prayers written and left in this sacred spot to ascend to God, the Eternal One.

Jerusalem and its Temple were destroyed in 70 AD by the Romans, which also marked the beginning of the Jewish Diaspora. During the Ottoman Period in the early 16th century, the wall became the Jews' chief place of pilgrimage, where they came to lament the destruction of the Temple. Sultan Suleiman the Magnificent ordered a fortress-wall built around Jerusalem, which remains to this day surrounding the Old City. After the Six Day War, the Israelis created the huge Western Wall Plaza where visitors and the faithful come. There is a long history of conquests associated with Jerusalem, but the Wall is now available to visitors of all faiths to come and silently pray. It is also used for public gatherings such as swearing-in ceremonies for soldiers of the Israeli defense system, bar mitzvahs and other religious celebrations.

Leaving the area, we once again heard the sound of the call to prayer emanating from the region of the Dome of the Rock, which sits on the original site of the Temple. Walking along, we saw a stone-arched tunnel where there used to be a valley. The destroyed rubble left in the valley by the Romans eventually became a walkway. At one time, there was an overpass known as the Bridge of the Priests leading to the tunnel over the valley.

We walked a portion of the Via Dolorosa, but were unable to envision the events that occurred along its way 2,000 years ago. There were no priests or pilgrims carrying crosses mourning the death of Jesus this day. Instead, the flat-stoned narrow street was noisy with peddlers, residents and children, often little boys with toy guns or little girls dressed in their holiday finest for a celebration that day. Electric wires strung like Christmas lights along the arched tunnels and over the lintels of what may have been apartment buildings added to the modern flavor of a city steeped in ancient history. People wearing contemporary fashions mingled with others dressed in the traditional long-flowing garb of the region. Combined with the sounds of electric saws, cars and children, Jerusalem once again provided a backdrop for which I was not prepared.

From there we walked to the sizeable archeological dig at the Pool of Bethesda which we were told was absolutely the location of the wondrous event (John, chapter 5:1-15) in which Jesus healed the paralytic. We were also told this was the only authentic location we would visit on our tour of the city. The pool area with its numerous platforms, stone buildings and arched doors enabled one to visualize the crowded conditions of long ago, when throngs of the infirm lay waiting for the angel of the Lord to "stir the waters." Because it extends from street level to much lower depths, the fascinating scene permitted one to "look down" into 2,000-year-old history, providing a panoramic view of the site of a miraculous healing by Jesus.

Imagine if you can, Jerusalem at the time of Jesus—a bustling, Roman-occupied city of approximately 50,000. From the numerous gates in the immense wall that surrounds the city, narrow crowded streets eventually lead to the magnificent Temple where daily prayers and sacrifices are offered. The sounds of priests praising the Lord resonate with shofars, bleating sheep and cooing doves fluttering in cages; all mingle with the scent of incense and burning sacrifices at the altar. Jesus walks by and stops to talk to a man carrying a rolled-up sleeping mat. It is the one He had healed only hours ago at the pool just outside the Sheep Gate, the one interrogated by the Jewish leaders at the Temple and accused of sin for carrying a mat on the Sabbath. When their conversation ends, the Bible tells us the man went to find the leaders and told them it was Jesus who had healed him.

Miracles are still happening just around the corner, but often no one is aware. It may be that you are not discerning of the miracles in your life and if this is true, stop for a moment, come away from the sights and sounds of the everyday—concentrate on the miracle of healing that took place at the Pool of Bethesda close to the Sheep Gate one Sabbath day. God will bring to your mind events you perhaps have forgotten. Today you can meet with Him and talk about it, just as the man at the Temple grounds did. Then follow his example and go—tell others what Christ has done for you!

Jesus did many other things as well. If every one of them were written down, I suppose that even the whole world would not have room for the books that would be written.

John 21:25, NIV

9. YAD VASHEM

To them I will give within my temple and its walls
a memorial and a name better than sons and
daughters; I will give them an everlasting
name that will not be cut off.

Isaiah 56:5, NIV

The Yad Vashem in Jerusalem is Israel's memorial to the six million people who died at the cruel hands of the Nazis during World War II. Located on the Hill of Remembrance on the western edge of the city, it was founded in 1953 when a law was passed by Israel's parliament, the Knesset. Its name is taken from the above Scripture, the words "yad" and "vashem" in Hebrew meaning memorial and name respectively.

Going to Yad Vashem took all of my courage. Reading books and watching movies had never seemed enough and after many years spent reading of the Nazi atrocities committed against the Jews, I wanted to honor those who perished by visiting the Holocaust Memorial. I never comprehended how unprepared I was for the shocking reality of it all until I was immersed in the sights and sounds of this place. I had repeatedly asked around for a companion to accompany me, but no one seemed to have the time or inclination to go. Eventually, a friend reluctantly agreed to go with me on the bus trip across Jerusalem.

The sun blazed hot as we exited the bus, but it felt hotter still as we approached the grounds—somehow it seemed fitting. I didn't take many photographs, but my camera for some unknown reason didn't pick up the natural colors that day; instead, each of the developed pictures were in various

45

flaming shades of orange, red and yellow. I believe the fiery orange-red shades of the photos brought to life the mindlessness of war and of the cruel persecution, anguish and death the victims of the Holocaust endured.

There are no words adequate to describe the utter sadness and emotional rejection I felt as we walked past the Torah Memorial Sculpture, a skeletal iron fence sculpture fashioned in the likeness of those whose skin and bones were all that was left at the end of the war. Made in the form of barbed wire, yet composed of emaciated heads attached to long shafts of bones which jutted at all angles from their barb-like prison, it articulated unspeakable horror to the viewer.

Upon entering the main buildings, my senses were again assaulted by the Holocaust reality as never before. My mind twisted and turned in a vain attempt to escape the images preserved in this place. My stomach roiled as I viewed the vast, towering mounds of children's shoes, exactly as they would have been piled at Auschwitz, Birkenau and hundreds of other torture camps. The innocent were left with nothing…not their hair, their clothes and valuables, their toys and baby dolls, not even their teeth and glasses. Everything belonging to *all* of the victims was cruelly taken and recycled for despicable use by the Reich. These depictions remain to this day my most vivid recollection of my time spent at the memorial.

There are countless books and websites available for those who feel they would want to learn more and thus honor those millions of innocents…they must not be forgotten. As long as there are memorials such as this, we cannot forget. Personally, my mind is seared with the vision of a mountain of little shoes and the human skeleton-like barbed wire fence. My blood-orange photographs taken in 1988 will forever hold me captive.

We must continue to remember the faces of the victims of hatred, fear and war, and be ever vigilant, not turning our face away. Man continues in his cruelty and hatred, yet we must never stop praying for the peace that God has promised.

*Never again will they hunger; never again will
they thirst. The sun will not beat upon them,
nor any scorching heat. For the Lamb at the
center of the throne will be their shepherd;
He will lead them to springs of living
water. And God will wipe away
every tear from their eyes.*

Revelation 7:16-17, NIV

10. ABBA

God also said to Moses, "Say to the Israelites, 'The LORD, the God of your fathers—the God of Abraham, the God of Isaac and the God of Jacob—has sent me to you. This is my name forever, the name by which I am to be remembered from generation to generation.'"

Exodus 3:15, NIV

It is interesting to note that our post-sunrise breakfast fare varied only slightly each day. Typically, we commenced our mornings with coffee, a variety of sliced and creamed cheeses, fish, cucumbers, shredded carrots, tomatoes and juice. Small loaves of bread, toast, matzos and boiled eggs were also included. After breakfast, there was time for a bit more sightseeing. Lunch was on our own and this day we hoped to have a snack in downtown Jerusalem...I couldn't wait, thinking perhaps I would sample a falafel—after all, I had been told they were delicious!

Following our brief downtown excursion would be a tour of a portion of the Israel Museum called the Shrine of the Book. This building houses the Dead Sea Scrolls, perhaps the most important archeological discovery in the history of Israel. Nothing could be more exciting than to see the ancient scrolls of Isaiah announcing the coming Messiah! The original scroll was found in 1947 by a youthful Bedouin shepherd in the region of Qumran, close to the Dead Sea, where the arid conditions perhaps provided a helping hand being conducive to the preservation of these precious letters.

We had but a minimum of free time, so the trip downtown was short. A few of us took a bus which was loaded with chattering school children, weary-looking moms and a couple of armed soldiers. I wondered if I could ever get accustomed to a military presence in my own home town in Ohio and decided that if it was necessary for security's sake, I would gladly endure their company. These were not youngsters playing soldier such as were seen along the Via Dolorosa, but well-trained men and women in service to their country. I later learned that each Israeli man or woman over the age of 18 (with some exceptions) must spend an allotted time in the Israel Defense Forces, three years for men and two years for women—dedicated, brave young people who deserve our admiration!

Eventually, we exited the bus and walked along a broad thoroughfare busy with shoppers, tourists and a plethora of enticing merchant stores and outdoor cafes. Flapping in the breeze were streamers of the blue and white Star of David and other Israeli symbols stretched overhead like clotheslines from one side of the avenue to the other as if in preparation for a party. We stopped for a luscious, steamy lamb pita sandwich, some much-needed cold water and a frozen yogurt at one of the outdoor cafes. One particular memory I enjoyed was that of an older gentleman who sat at a table which he had set up on the street, shouting out to passersby that he was selling "scratch" lottery tickets. All too soon, it was time to board a return bus in order to join the tour of the Shrine of the Book.

Exteriorly, the Shrine had been built to resemble the lid of a clay jar, similar to the ones in which some of the earliest scrolls were found. Within, the starkness of the modern architectural design of the building provided me with a swarm of feelings at once suggesting the contemporary and the traditional, the current and the ancient. I remembered the guide's advice given earlier in the week that in Israel, there are always at least two meanings to every word—I would see this adage resurrected again and again during my trip.

The most valued items on display at the Shrine were two copies of the book of Isaiah, more than 1,000 years older than any others known to be in existence. Portions of the book of Isaiah were encased within a symbolic likeness of an ancient scroll, its lustrous mahogany handle reaching toward the epicenter of the circular, vaulted ceiling. This area was elevated from the ground floor of the dome-like building and was reached by climbing the broad stark steps leading to it.

It was at the base of the steps that I was again transported to another season of time, as so often can happen in this land of the Bible. A father and his son had come down the stairs shortly after I had. The little boy went to a nearby seating area and inquired of his father. Of course, I didn't understand what he was saying, but he was definitely asking a question.

"Abba?"

The kindly young father looked down attentively toward his child and responded with what I can only assume would be a natural reply. "Yes, son? What is it you are wanting?"

I was entranced by the interaction I observed in those few minutes and have never forgotten the love and tenderness between father and son that I beheld there in that brief moment in time. It was a lesson not learned from tutors, tour guides or teachers, but rather one learned from the greatest book of all—the Bible.

Listen to Jesus, as He agonizes in the Garden of Gethsemane on the night He was betrayed when He inquired of His Father.

> *"Abba, Father," he said, "everything is possible*
> *for you. Take this cup from me. Yet not what*
> *I will, but what you will."*

Mark 14:36, NIV

Some have said Abba can be loosely defined by the childlike form for Father—that is to say, *Daddy.* Some disagree. I love the intimacy the form would imply if used in the childlike context. So many of us have never had that personal relationship with our earthly father, so the inviting term of "Daddy" beckons us to the knee that perhaps we have never sat upon, the broad chest we have never leaned against or the strong protective arms which have never embraced us. Our Father in Heaven warmly invites us into His lap where He can enfold us in His love. I pray that none of us ever feel we are too old, too sophisticated or too strong emotionally to deny ourselves the blessing of His loving embrace.

Because you are sons, God sent the Spirit
of his Son into our hearts, the Spirit who
calls out, "Abba, Father."

Galatians 4:6, NIV

No longer are we held captive to old laws and constraints. Because of the precious blood shed by our Lord Jesus, we too can come to the Father in full assurance of His acceptance and pleasure in us, not because of who we are, but because Christ made the way for us to boldly enter the throne of God. There we can come for solace, comfort, companionship and security.

For you did not receive a spirit that makes you a slave
again to fear, but you received the Spirit of sonship.
And by him we cry, "Abba, Father." The Spirit
himself testifies with our spirit that we are
God's children.

Romans 8:15-16, NIV

11. GETHSEMANE

*Do not be far from me, for trouble is
near and there is no one to help.*

Psalm 22:11, NIV

On the first day of the Passover, when Jesus and the
disciples ate the ritual dinner which commemorated the
exodus of the Jews from Egypt, He instituted something new
to the ancient ceremony. As they ate the lamb, bitter herbs
and unleavened bread, and drank the wine, Jesus foretold of
His ensuing betrayal by one of them. He told them also of
His coming death, likening His body to the bread and His
blood to the wine which they shared that evening.

After this, they sang a hymn, then walked along the
narrow streets of the city through the eastern gate and
across the Kidron ravine to a place they often went for
prayer—an olive grove located at the foot of the Mount of
Olives.

From our parking spot, we walked down a steep hill and
followed along the same general direction until we came to
the Garden of Gethsemane (Aramaic for olive press). Behind
a stone wall resplendent with cascades of fuchsia
bougainvillea, we found a most peaceful garden populated
with many ancient, silvery-green-leafed olive trees, some of
which may have been present 2,000 years ago. Although no
one can be sure if any of these trees could have existed
during the time of Jesus, it is quite possible, as they are
known to regenerate from the root system even if the tree
structure itself has been damaged. The thicker and more
gnarled the trunk, the older the tree will be, so it is within
reason that the branches of some of these aged, broad-based

olive trees could have provided the canopy under which the Lord prayed on the last night of His earthly life.

The current Church of Gethsemane was built in the 1920's atop the site of a 4th century Byzantine church which had long been a focal point for Christian pilgrims who sought to meditate the anguish Jesus suffered there. The building's elegant façade of immense arches and supporting pillars is capped with a beautiful mosaic depiction of the biblical story of the Garden of Gethsemane.

Within the beautiful church, it was quiet and dark with stained-glass windows formed in a cross—so very peaceful! A wrought iron railing in the form of the crown of thorns that pierced our Lord's head, surrounded the rock of agony where Jesus is said to have prayed. The Bible tells us He prayed with such fervency that great drops of blood came from His brow. I felt very close to Jesus there in the solemn dimness—more so than at any location I had visited thus far.

As I knelt and prayed for my loved ones and the world, I also thanked Jesus for His love and suffering for me—for all of us. Overwhelmed with sorrow for all I had ever done to hurt and sadden Him, I silently shed tears of remorse and asked forgiveness of the One who had loved me enough to proceed, perhaps from this very spot, to the many unjust trials which eventually ended at the "Place of the Skull" outside the city.

As the bloodied and battered Savior struggled to carry the cross, He was mocked and spat upon for *me*—for *Carol*, and it was as if I were the only person who had ever existed. I cannot fathom God's love for me. *I* should have been the one carrying that cross; *I* should have endured the scorn, the ridicule and the torture of this unspeakable death, not Jesus. Thank you, dear Lord, for Your willingness to die for me. I pray that I will serve You well until the day that I take my last breath—that you will be honored by my life. May it be a testimony of all You have done for me.

Dear reader, as you spend some time with Jesus just now here in the Garden of Gethsemane, look within your heart. Ask forgiveness if you already haven't and offer yourself to Him without reservation. Welcome Him into your heart; renew your commitment to live a life that will give Him glory. He will fill your heart with unfathomable peace.

During the days of Jesus' life on earth, he offered up prayers and petitions with loud cries and tears to the one who could save him from death, and he was heard because of his reverent submission.

Hebrews 5:7, NIV

12. THE GARDENER

*The LORD will guide you always; he will satisfy your
needs in a sun-scorched land and will strengthen
your frame. You will be like a well-watered
garden, like a spring whose waters
never fail.*

Isaiah 58:11, NIV

My eyes were drawn in an irresistible way to the
gardener. He was not standing tall and erect, but instead
was bent over in a gentle, kindly manner as if tending to
something much beloved. His hands were wrapped around
the handle of a straw broom, its bristles well worn to a sharp
angle and curled at the tips. I was intrigued by his
appearance and with the exception of his clothing, I realized
that I could easily have been observing a gardener 2,000
years back in history.

He was dressed in lightweight, loose-fitting khaki-
colored pants and an olive-green, long-sleeved shirt, rolled
up to his elbows. The white scarf covering his head flowed
gently down and across his shoulders and back. Holding it in
place was a twisted black cloth rope of sorts, which fit over
the crown of his head.

My absorption was fleeting because I was with the tour
group, but I did manage to snap a picture of him as he
worked. I was struck by the peacefulness that surrounded
me and also by the reverent way in which he tended the
stone pathways which meandered through the garden area.
It was so quiet, so lovely there that for a brief moment, I felt
as though I was alone with him. My thoughts transported
me back in time to another woman's encounter with a

gardener, perhaps in this same location, for I was not standing in just any garden—I was in the area which contains the Garden Tomb, a site that some say could be the traditional location of Christ's burial. British General Charles Gordon, while visiting Jerusalem in 1883, reviewed the geography of an area quite close to the Damascus Gate. There he not only saw the limestone, skull-like outcropping we know as Golgotha, but also discovered a tomb of the Roman period not too far west of Golgotha which is now known as Gordon's Tomb.

However, my rapt attention at this time was not toward the tomb, which was within my scope of vision, but was instead focused upon contemplation of the gardener and his quiet reverential care of the garden in which the tomb was located. Not a sound disturbed my thoughts except perhaps the distant, soft whisperings of the pilgrims who followed one another down the worn stone steps leading to the burial place.

A sense of holiness pervaded the garden. Its tropical plant life and sweet-smelling flowers along with a scattering of soundless, bouncing butterflies settling here and there drinking nectar, added to the serenity of the moment.

Being well aware that this was but another "traditional" holy site, neither authenticated nor sanctified, I nevertheless was brought to a state of deep contemplation regarding the One who might have been buried there. It was a perfect setting to envision Christ's gentle approach to Mary as she was about to leave the empty tomb, devastated that her Lord's body was not there. Believing it had been carried away, she began to cry. A soft, loving voice called her name…*"Mary"* (John 20:16). At first, she thought it was a gardener who had spoken to her, but when she heard the sound of her name as it was spoken, she turned and immediately recognized Him.

I wonder…would I…do I…hear His soft, gentle voice in the midst of my tears when all around me seems to be crumbling and my hope disintegrating? I must pray that I will *hear and recognize* His voice when He calls my name in the garden of my life. In times of sunshine, storms or drought, whether being pruned or disturbed by the upheaval of the earth around my roots, I want to heed His voice, trusting Him to bring me to my full potential as one of His servants, regardless of my own fears and anxieties.

The Master Gardener attends to us lovingly, having all knowledge of our needs. When I was living in southern California some years ago, I was responsible for care of a small patio area filled with plants and trees that thrive in that hot and arid location. Being from the Midwest, I was mystified by their constant need for water and their only occasional need for trimming. I was so fearful of doing damage to the plants. After a month or so of meticulous attention to the tropical flora, I panicked when many of them appeared to have withered and died. I had tried my best, yet not knowing the region or the peculiarities of the individual plants' needs, I had, in my zealous gardening, either watered them too much or not enough—I did not know which. It seemed that the few people I asked had no understanding of my plight, for they did not seem to be the least bit concerned. Of course, I was unaware that many of the plants were just taking a temporary rest until their next flowering season arrived. I finally thought to call a friend in Ohio who is a master gardener. Her advice on the particular plants I was tending was invaluable. I quickly recognized the importance of heeding and trusting the knowledge of one who is a master in the field of horticulture.

The incident also served to remind me of the day I spent near the Garden Tomb in Jerusalem and of the devoted gardener I have described. He understood his job and performed it with the knowledge required to tend that serene plot of land. I was reminded also of the meticulous care that God displays as He tends to each of our lives. He knows exactly when to water, when to turn the dirt, when to allow us to seemingly become withered and dry (permitting us to develop our roots). God also knows when to prune, knowing full-well that at the perfect time, we will bloom forth with sweet, aromatic blossoms and soon we will produce the fruit of His Spirit.

I am the true vine, and my Father is the gardener. He cuts off every branch in me that bears no fruit, while every branch that does bear fruit he prunes so that it will be even more fruitful.

John 15:1-2, NIV

13. THE WAY OF THE SEA

Nevertheless, there will be no more gloom for those
who were in distress. In the past he humbled the
land of Zebulun and the land of Naphtali, but in
the future he will honor Galilee of the Gentiles,
by the way of the sea, along the Jordan.

Isaiah 9:1, NIV

The Way of the Sea or Via Maris was an ancient trade route across Palestine (then Canaan) to Egypt from Mesopotamia, cutting through the Carmel Range at the strategic city of Megiddo which guarded this crucial mountain pass. Here it split into two main branches, one leading to Tyre and Sidon and the other an inland route through the Jezreel Valley to the Sea of Galilee. There is a reference to "the Way of the Sea" in the prophetic words of Isaiah above.

Three cities along the Via Maris were especially important due to their advantageous locations, Megiddo being the first. Second was Hazor, north of the Sea of Galilee, which guarded a narrow section of the road in the Rift Valley. Lastly, Gezer was strategically situated at the junction of the international coastal highway and the highway connecting it with Jerusalem. It also connected the Via Maris to an east-west road that led to Jericho.

Because of these vital trade routes, Palestine was constantly visited by travelers, nomad shepherds and warring peoples. It was along the northeastern trade route of the Way of the Sea that Joseph was sold into slavery to an Ishmaelite caravan headed for Egypt. Many of Canaan's walled cities were located along these strategic routes.

Joseph was probably sold into slavery by his brothers to a group of traders traveling along the Way of the Sea.

Often in our travels through the Holy Land, we would visit locations which are now no more than decaying remnants of what were once important cities along the Way of the Sea. These were frequently scenes of the bloody history of man protecting his own, be it property claims or simply strategic locations. The rugged, yet varying terrain of Israel lends itself to such warfare engagements and its important location along the trade routes made it all the more imperative to protect it.

Considering its size, it was not hard to envision driving only a few miles before arriving at one and then another location of biblical significance. In fact, it is astounding when one looks at a pilgrim's map of modern Israel, for then its size seems to diminish even more. A land with such a rich history which occurred over the millennia has many tales to tell. Locations we have heard about all of our lives overlap. Cities, villages and locations were given new names by the conquerors and yet, the history stands firm, confirmed over again by the Scriptures and archeology.

Let us thank God for providing us with the most fascinating history book ever written, one which has been inspired by His Holy Spirit and is accurate in its facts. The harmony found within its 66 books, written over thousands of years by many scribes, is astounding and although many have tried to discredit it, none have succeeded. As you travel its ancient highways and paths, seek to know more of God and His Holy Land each day, for He has much to tell.

*All Scripture is God-breathed and is useful for teaching,
rebuking, correcting and training in righteousness.*

2 Timothy 3:16, NIV

14. BETHLEHEM – CITY OF DAVID, HOUSE OF BREAD

But you, Bethlehem Ephrathah, though you are
small among the clans of Judah, out of you
will come for me one who will be ruler
over Israel, whose origins are from
of old, from ancient times.

Micah 5:2, NIV

As we prepared to leave the city of Jerusalem, it was interesting to note that the little city of Bethlehem lies only five miles south of the Holy City. In 1988, it was in the West Bank...60,000 Palestinians under Israeli rule. It was a much shorter ride from Jerusalem to Bethlehem than one would think and no sooner had we left the outskirts of the city than the driver was pointing out to us Rachael's tomb on the right and the Shepherd's Field on the left.

Bethlehem sits on a limestone ridge along the main highway to Hebron and Egypt and it was here that Rachael died giving birth to Benjamin (Genesis 48:7) so many centuries ago. At that time, it was called Ephrath (Genesis 35:16-21). Later, it was there Ruth gleaned the fields of Boaz, son of Rahab (Ruth 1). They eventually married and she became the great-grandmother of King David (Ruth 4). Bethlehem was also the birthplace of Jesse, the father of the shepherd David and also the birthplace of David himself (1 Samuel 16). It was here in this humble town that David was anointed by Samuel as the shepherd-king of Israel (1 Samuel 16:1-13) and here also was to be the birthplace of Jesus, the Messiah, the Everlasting King (Micah 5:2).

Bethlehem was a small, but busy town in the time of Joseph and Mary. Although only several hundred people made their home there, caravans en route to Egypt often stopped for rest in Bethlehem, swelling the population since an inn had been built in the time of David nearly 1,000 years before. Bethlehem was also a farming community surrounded by productive wheat and barley fields, olive groves and grazing pastures suitable for sheep. Its harvests were abundant and perhaps that is why it was sometimes referred to as the "house of bread." How amazing that Jesus the *Bread of Life* was born in this tiny village of crucial position in biblical history.

As they passed through the entrance to the town, Mary and Joseph would have seen armed Roman soldiers guarding the gate. As they reached the top of the steep hill, they encountered the busyness of Bethlehem's marketplace. The tiny town would have been crowded and noisy with its many visitors who had traveled to register and pay their taxes to King Herod. Though it was but a humble Judean village, Bethlehem had been chosen by God to be the birthplace of His Son Jesus.

> *But you, O Bethlehem Ephrathah, are only a small village*
> *among all the people of Judah. Yet a ruler of Israel*
> *will come from you, one whose origins are from*
> *the distant past.*

> Micah 5:2, NLT

Things weren't much different in May 1988 when we arrived in Bethlehem. My heart sank as I searched for the quiet little town of which we sing in our beloved Christmas songs. It was not the "little town of Bethlehem" and it was certainly not quiet and still. I yearned for the deepness of the midnight sky I had always envisioned; the one filled with heavenly angels heralding the arrival of our Savior Jesus. I was at once bewildered and saddened by the reality of today's Bethlehem, even though our guide had given us ample warning. Israeli soldiers, tanks and jeeps were everywhere, even parked on the famous Manger Square. Alongside the soldiers were Palestinians hawking their wares—rosaries, golden necklaces, jeweled bracelets and postcards of the city and its famous Church of the Nativity.

Our guide warned us as we stepped down from the bus to remember that we were here to see the Holy Place and to keep our eyes on the object of our pilgrimage that day.

The Church of the Nativity sits across the square, towering above the place where Emperor Constantine's mother, Helena, believed that Jesus was born. The oldest building in Christendom was built by Constantine in 330 AD over a cave-like room that is said to be the actual manger room in which Christ was born. The entrance to the Church was lowered possibly during the Middle Ages to prevent the invaders from riding their horses into the holy place, desecrating it by using the building as a stable for their horses. It has remained lowered since that time and, therefore, one must bend low in order to enter the church even to this day. I thought to myself that we must also bend low and humble ourselves in order to enter into that wonderful relationship with the Holy Child of Bethlehem and the King of our lives.

Before you can enter the doorway to the church, however, you must walk across the square past soldiers with their weapons of war and merchants with their enticing lures. "Is it the Holy place that you seek? Keep your eyes on the doorway then or you will be distracted," our guide warned us. It was indeed difficult to exit the security of the bus and try to fend our way through the many soldiers, tanks and trucks. We were not accustomed to such tangible evidences of war. Even more distracting, however, were the immediate assaults to the senses by the merchants, many speaking a different language, attempting to sell their jewelry to you. Necklaces and bracelets dangled from every finger and wrist as arms were thrust toward us. Prices in shekels were shouted out to our neighbors as we made our way toward the church. *"Keep your eyes on that which you have come to see"* echoed in my head as I steadfastly refused the offers to buy beautiful jewelry and other gifts. I stared straight ahead at the tiny doorway across the square thinking I would never get there. The distraction was indeed tremendous to me.

The Lord reminded me later that this scene on Manger Square very much resembles our life here on earth, for it is full of enticements and temptations for the "better things"... money, position, power...whatever one's god may be. On the other hand, we can also be distracted by the tumult of our lives, which may be marked by illness, war, financial reversals or loss of loved ones. Any of these earthly problems and a host of others can effectively keep us asking God why He allows these things to happen. Either way, our eyes are kept from seeing God and also from our goal of one day spending eternity with Him.

Who is it that you seek?

Let us fix our eyes on Jesus, the author and perfecter of our faith, who for the joy set before him endured the cross, scorning its shame, and sat down at the right hand of the throne of God.

Hebrews 12:2, NIV

Beware of, and resist, those things that work against your trust in Him. Enter the Way humbly and as untainted by the world as you can be.

15. A STOP ALONG THE WAY

Have I not commanded you? Be strong and
courageous. Do not be terrified; do not be
discouraged, for the LORD your God
will be with you wherever you go.

Joshua 1:9, NIV

"There is in all the world nothing quite like the contrast between the mountain city of Jerusalem, over 2,500 feet above sea level and the Jordan Valley, only 23 miles away, sunk in a hot trench 1,300 feet below the sea...." This quote is from the book, *In Search of the Holy Land* by H. V. Morton.

Rather interesting, I thought, that it is a steep descent of only 14 miles distance from the City of God to the lowest point on earth! We were heading into the dry and barren wilderness—the same wilderness David hid in as he tried to escape the jealous King Saul and where Jesus, alone for 40 days, was tempted by Satan after His baptism in the Jordan River. It was indeed a desolate, lonely environment through which to travel.

Along the way, we stopped at the Good Samaritan Inn, the only stopping place on this road. It was most likely the site of an earlier inn which Jesus used in the parable of the Good Samaritan. The way was dangerous and many travelers were robbed, hurt and even killed along its route. Across the road from the inn, hill on a hill, was what remained of a Roman lookout station, a spot from which to watch for thieves and robbers.

It is in this treacherous location that we meet the (much-despised) Samaritan in Jesus' parable. He was the only person who offered to help an injured man, putting him on his donkey and taking him to the inn where he agreed to pay the entire bill for his care. The parable presents to us a likeness of Jesus (often a much-despised man), who provides help, healing, relief and salvation to each of us. He too, has offered (and has already paid) the complete cost of our eternal salvation.

Many times in our lives, we also seem to be alone in the wilderness. Perhaps we've wandered away from God, heading into deeper and deeper valleys until we feel we've reached the "lowest place on earth." Travel along this road away from Jerusalem leads to such a place, the Dead Sea, which can be seen as a beautiful blue body of water from a few miles distance. Relief and sustenance from this uninhabited, parched location seem so close, but as beautiful as it appears, the sea is without life and to drink of its salt and bromide content would lead to death—to continue in this direction would be lethal.

On the other hand, we can choose to turn our backs to the Dead Sea and walk westward again toward Jerusalem. The terrain is just as rough and dry, but there is a nearby oasis at Jericho and heading into the Dead Sea is the River Jordan with its fresh water. Not too far in the distance, high on the mountains, can be seen Jerusalem, the Holy City of God. We see the opportunity to live rather than to perish as a reality!

Let's stop a moment and consider that the same rough road leads in both directions, one *away* from God to despair and death and one *toward* God, our everlasting hope and salvation. For each of us, it is a matter of choice as to which direction we take on our life's travels. We too will have opportunities to minister the love of God as we walk the wilderness of our lives. God has promised He would never leave us or forsake us (Hebrews 13:5) and we need to remember that we do not travel along this hot and dusty way alone. His promises are true; we can always rely on them. It is also good to remind ourselves of what He has done for ourselves and others in the past. The Bible is filled with stories of deliverance!

When the road is rough and your feet are tired...when you're thirsty and you feel so all alone, remember this great example, for we don't travel the road alone, not even for one second!

He goes on ahead of them.

John 10:4, NIV

16. REEBOKS AND WATER BOTTLES

O God, you are my God, earnestly I seek you;
my soul thirsts for you, my body longs for
you, in a dry and weary land where
there is no water.

Psalm 63:1, NIV

"Mom!"

Laura's voice was upsetting my concentration. I was packing my suitcases for a two-week trip to the Holy Land and felt I didn't need the advice of a drama queen. My thirteen-year-old daughter Laura was obviously exasperated with me and I was being equally stubborn in return.

"No, Laura, for the last time, I am *not* going to buy an expensive pair of Reeboks and that's final! Please! Stop asking me about it!"

My trip to Israel was only a day away, but I still hadn't bought any walking shoes. The simple truth was that I did not want to spend any more money than I already had in preparation for the journey. (I was ignoring the fact that although I'd had no money to finance the trip, God had amazingly provided every dollar required including $200 spending money.) My frugal nature just wouldn't permit me to invest in a solid, comfortable pair of shoes. Laura was unrelenting, however, and eventually I succumbed to her admonition. (If you have never been admonished by a teenage daughter, be forewarned! It's hard to take!) As a teen, she was constantly asking for name-brand shoes, name-brand clothes, name-brand skin care products and on and on. Why, she even demanded (or tried to demand) that I buy her bottled water! I, who was raised on free, fresh-from-the-ground pure, cold well water, was aghast! Oh, I grant you, city water tasted incredibly like a science lab smelled, but nevertheless...bottled water? Another name-brand extravagance we could live without, I declared.

However, time was running out and I did need to purchase some walking shoes. Reluctantly, I gathered my courage to spend some money on myself, as Laura had suggested. Shoe stores abound in malls and it frustrated me that I had so little time to search for the perfect bargain! At Laura's insistence, I tried on a pair of Reeboks, all the while thinking of the resultant deprivation I would have to endure to make up for the cost. I sighed as I paid for the shoes and thought to myself, well, no souvenirs for me, no falafel sandwiches... I'll have to drink lots of water instead. (Water is not my favorite choice of beverage, but it would be free and easy on the pocketbook.)

That evening, as I finished packing, I tried out my new shoes. I couldn't believe it! I felt as though I was walking on air, just as the advertisers had promised. Incredible comfort! I was hooked!

Two days later, I arrived at the Ben Gurion International Airport near Tel Aviv...unfortunately sans luggage. It arrived safely three days later...and just in time, too! Already, a previous half-day excursion had proven to me the need for foot comfort, but the next one, an all-day trip to the lowest point on earth (the Dead Sea), would clinch my awareness of Laura's wisdom. I gratefully stepped into my new "name-brand" walking shoes that morning and thanked God for the arrival of my luggage, the contents of which included the object of my daughter's sage advice.

The following is an excerpt from my journal written on that blistering hot day:

"A walk from where the bus is parked to the Dead Sea is but a short distance. However, the extreme heat is overwhelming and all-encompassing. The path feels steeper, the rocks jagged and unyielding, the thirst more intense...a good place to contemplate the need for proper walking shoes and the desire for Jesus' offering of Living Water."

Earlier that day at the hotel, we had queued up for...you guessed it...bottles of water!

I, who had scorned at plastic water bottles less than a week prior, now eagerly brought the container to my parched lips. Oh, I was beginning to understand something! Here in this harsh and arid place where no creature lives, I absolutely *needed* life-giving water! I loved it, craved it, needed it desperately...and God smiled as He reminded me that I must also crave the Living Water, free for the asking, in order to navigate my way through the cruel and rocky paths of my life. I must never forget to nourish my spirit with this precious gift again.

But whoever drinks the water I give him will never thirst.
Indeed, the water I give him will become in him a spring
of water welling up to eternal life.

John 4:14, NIV

In a spiritual application, it is easy to understand His message to me that day. Try to visualize being in this searing, arid location with its easy access to what appears to be satisfying, life-giving water. The Dead Sea, for all of its beauty, offers no life at all. Jesus has given us assurance of quenched thirst—it is free for the asking.

Do not disdain that which you need to survive!

Wear shoes that are able to speed you on as you preach the
Good News of peace with God.

Ephesians 6:15, TLB

17. JERICHO

Then Moses climbed Mount Nebo from the plains of Moab to the top of Pisgah, across from Jericho. There the LORD showed him the whole land—from Gilead to Dan, all of Naphtali, the territory of Ephraim and Manasseh, all the land of Judah as far as the western sea, the Negev and the whole region from the Valley of Jericho, the City of Palms, as far as Zoar.

Deuteronomy 34:1-3, NIV

After leaving the Good Samaritan Inn, we continued through the wilderness and on to the most ancient city in the world and site of Joshua's most famous conquest. Soon we saw Jericho resting in an oasis valley, resplendently green with vineyards and palm trees—lushness in the wilderness!

Further along was the treed area of the Jordan River, site of Joshua's crossing and traditional site of Jesus' baptism. We were on the north and western side of the Jordan with date plantations visible, the Dead Sea only eight miles away. Across the sea was Mount Nebo where Moses died. In modern Jericho, we viewed the huge sycamore tree, the traditional place of Zacchaeus' fame.

The Exodus from Egypt led by Moses lasted about 40 years. Although the Israelites neared the Promised Land within a year, they did not trust God enough to enter and as punishment, God declared that with the exception of two of the spies, Joshua and Caleb, all adults had to die before the Israelites could enter the land.

In this desert your bodies will fall—every one of you twenty years old or more who was counted in the census and who has grumbled against me.

Numbers 14:29, NIV

Joshua, as you know, became Moses' successor and led the Israelites across the Jordan River, the first conquest being the fortified city of Jericho. According to modern archeological research, the city was already several thousand years old at the time of its defeat by Joshua. Jericho was situated several miles northwest of where the Israelites crossed the Jordan, just north of the Dead Sea. Even then, it was located atop a steep mound—or tell—composed of layers of remains from all its previous settlements.

Considering its heavy fortification, it was most likely a border outpost during this time, for it stood on one of the few roads connecting the Via Maris, a major trade route to the west, and the north-south King's Highway. It also had the strategic advantage of being near to the fords of the Jordan. The name Jericho means "its sweet smell" although it also was often called the "city of palms." More than 800 feet below sea level, Jericho is the oldest city known to man, dating back to 9,000 BC according to research and archeologists' reports. At approximately 846 feet below sea level, it is also the lowest city in the world.

We visited the archeological digs of ancient Jericho and were told by our guide about the psychological warfare that took place here, where only Rehab's home was safe. Historians say the great battle took place around 1240 BC, although 1440 BC fits more with the archeology. We looked down into the tower built of stones at the entrance and saw a spiral stairway which led into the depths of ancient Jericho. *The Source*, a fascinating book by James Michener, tells the complete story of a similar, but fictional city from its earliest beginnings to modern times based on the findings of modern-day archeologists. As only Mr. Michener can do, its 909 pages are filled with exciting historical accounts of the Holy Land, peppered with intriguing fictional and non-fictional characters.

Wind, rain and the centuries have buried many of the tell sites with earth and grass, giving them a hill-like appearance. Excavating sites such as this in a scientific manner involves many years, sometimes even a lifetime for dedicated archeologists. Extensive digs have taken place at the mound known as Tel Es-Sultan, the most famous being those conducted in the 1950's by renowned archeologist Kathleen Kenyon. Excavations of 1929-1936 found that the wall was actually a double one with walls approximately 15 feet apart and linked together—Rahab's home was on the wall of the city, a very convenient location indeed.

So she let them down by a rope through the window, for the house she lived in was part of the city wall.

Joshua 2:15, NIV

New Testament Jericho, the one to which Jesus walked and where Zacchaeus climbed a sycamore tree to see the One who had healed a blind man, was about a mile southwest of the ruins of Old Testament Jericho. Here Herod the Great had built a large palace and it is here that he died. Behind, up on a hill, are a monastery and also the traditional site of the Mount of Temptation.

Would you be willing to climb a tree just to see Jesus? Would you even climb a mountain to meet with Him? Think about the opportunities you have had over your lifetime to spend some very personal time with Jesus...just you and Him. Did you use the time wisely or were you distracted? So many times life gets in the way of our best intentions, but He is still ready and waiting. Perhaps today is the day set aside just for you!

When Jesus reached the spot, he looked up and said to him, "Zacchaeus, come down immediately. I must stay at your house today." So he came down at once and welcomed him gladly.

Luke 19:5-6, NIV

18. UP THE MOUNTAIN

Be ready in the morning, and then come up on
Mount Sinai. Present yourself to me there on
top of the mountain.

Exodus 34:2, NIV

How important do you think it is to climb a mountain? Mountaineers often say they endure the hardships, rigors and risk of life and limb to climb a mountain "because it is there." This is a perfectly sensible answer if reaching the summit is your plan—nothing else matters when it comes to reaching that goal!

What about those of us who do not have that drive, that burning passion within us to "summit" the crest? Can we relate to the passion with which mountain climbers strive to reach their target? I think we can, for in our lifetime, in spite of everything, we will still have many mountains to scale. Reaching the top—in a figurative manner of speaking—can result in exhilaration and relief. What seemed insur-mountable has been conquered! We feel ecstatic, joyous and sometimes even proud! However, if given a choice, each of us would have exempted ourselves from the hardships required to reach that pinnacle.

When we undergo spiritual renewal, we frequently say we have had a mountaintop experience. We want to stay there forever, never letting go of the profound fullness we have come in contact with at that moment. In the land of the Bible, we read of many mountaintop events, not all of which are superlative, however. As an example, Abraham, as he obediently took his son up the mountain of Moriah, had to have been in spiritual anguish, but he had an appointment with God there in those heights. Moses' mountaintop experience also resulted in a monumental meeting with the Lord, as he stood on holy ground and received the Ten Commandments. Later, as he neared the end of his leadership journey to the Promised Land, Moses climbed from the plains of Moab to Pisgah Peak in Mount Nebo across from Jericho (Deuteronomy 34:1). After God pointed out to him the Promised Land, Moses died. The Bible says,

> *The Lord buried him in a valley near Beth-Peor*
> *in Moab, but no one knows the exact place.*
>
> Deuteronomy 34:6, TLB

Can you imagine God, our Creator, personally burying the man He chose to deliver His people out of bondage? Somehow, this scene cuts into my heart. I grieve for God. Moses, as a likeness of Jesus, gives me pause for consideration of the death of our true Deliverer being buried in a stone enclosure carved from rock bed by man.

Not too far from Jericho stands the traditional Mountain of Temptation, its craggy cliffs staggering upward to the sky. When our tour bus stopped to allow us time to contemplate Jesus' 40 days of temptation, I desperately wanted to climb the traditionally designated slopes. I remember it as arduous and steep on a scorching hot day. I climbed as high as I was able before the call to return to the bus beckoned me, although a barbed wire fence up ahead would have soon ended my climb anyway. I reluctantly relinquished my ascent, but not my thoughts.

Jesus, as we know, entered into a time of physical, mental and spiritual temptation immediately after His baptism in the Jordan River. What a mountaintop experience that must have been! Only the Triune God had known from the beginning that the day would arrive when Jesus would identify Himself with mankind, be baptized and authenticated as the Messiah by the presence of the Holy Spirit descending upon Him as a dove and the very voice of God declaring Him as His Son!

The Bible tells us in Matthew 4:1-11, that Jesus was *immediately* led by the Holy Spirit into the wilderness, where for 40 days and 40 nights Jesus was continually taunted and tested by Satan who twisted and distorted the Scriptures in a vain attempt to disprove Christ's deity. Jesus, humanly weakened by His fast, responded each time with the Word of God and eventually Satan went away and angels came and cared for Him.

What mountaintop are you experiencing today? Is it an exhilarating one in which you are filled to overflowing with God's love and the Holy Spirit's power? If so, it is a wonderful time to contemplate Scriptural truths about the overcoming life you are blessed with; but perhaps it is a mountaintop experience through which you are being tried and tested regarding your choice to be on the Lord's side. If so, take heart and join with Jesus, defying the enemy at all costs and seeing him for what he is—a liar, murderer and deceiver—one who will slyly distort God's Word in order to defeat you. Follow Jesus' example and be ready to speak Scriptural truths in rebuttal to Satan, for he has no power on the Mount of Temptation.

Take time to be alone with God, just as Jesus did.

...he went up on a mountainside by himself to pray.

Matthew 14:23, NIV

19. PUT YOUR FEET IN THE JORDAN

So when the people broke camp to cross the Jordan,
the priests carrying the ark of the covenant went
ahead of them. Now the Jordan is at flood stage
all during harvest. Yet as soon as the priests
who carried the ark reached the Jordan and
their feet touched the water's edge, the
water from upstream stopped flowing.

Joshua 3:14-16, NIV

In Genesis 13:10, we read of Abraham and Lot's decision to divide the grazing lands they had been sharing. After repeated arguments among their herdsmen, they felt it the best thing to do. Standing high on a hill, Lot looked over the fertile plains and the Jordan River. Abraham had given Lot first choice, for the entire area was "like the garden of Eden." Lot chose the beautiful country east of the river and Abraham then stayed on the west. The Lord told him to look in all four directions and told him that all the land he could see was to be a gift from God, promising him many descendants.

The LORD said to Abram after Lot had parted from
him, "Lift up your eyes from where you are and look
north and south, east and west. All the land that you
see I will give to you and your offspring forever. I will
make your offspring like the dust of the earth, so that
if anyone could count the dust, then your offspring
could be counted. Go, walk through the length and
breadth of the land, for I am giving it to you."

Genesis 13:14-17, NIV

Many years later, after bondage in Egypt, Joshua led the Israelites across the river to the Promised Land (Canaan then; Israel today). God gave the land to Abraham as a gift because of his faith...and here in this land would be born the Savior. When Joshua led the Israelites across the river, they also had to step out in faith, just as Abraham had done when he left his homeland in obedience and set out to an unknown place. After wandering 40 years in the desert, they were told to cross, not a placid flowing stream, but the flooding, raging Jordan River!

The Jordan begins in the Hula Valley in the north and follows a rather serpentine route southward about 75 miles until it reaches the Dead Sea. The Hebrew name *Jordan* literally means "descender" and it lives up to its name. Beginning 230 feet above sea level, it drops to 700 feet below sea level at about ten miles south of the Sea of Galilee. By the time it has reached the north end of the Dead Sea, the river has plunged to1,290 feet below sea level. Because of its meandering path, the river's 75-mile distance more than doubles.

During the spring thaws, the waters of the Jordan become a surging, rushing torrent, fordable in only two locations. One, near Jericho just north of the Dead Sea, is where Joshua crossed over; it was in the spring when the Jordan was overflowing! Imagine the faith required to obey God! A desert behind them, a flooding river to cross and a land to conquer on the other side! We can read in the book of Joshua how the Lord stopped the waters. As soon as the priests carrying the Ark of the Covenant put their feet in the Jordan, it allowed His people to cross on dry land (very reminiscent of the crossing of the Red Sea by their forebearers).

Although the site of Jesus' baptism is unclear, Christian tradition since at least the 6th century has named the Haljah Ford, east of Jericho, as the site. John's gospel says it took place in "Bethany, beyond the Jordan" (John 1:28). John the Baptist had been preaching to men to repent and turn to God, with baptism serving as a public announcement of a turning away from sin. It was already a Jewish custom to baptize Gentile converts, but John was baptizing Jews! In fact, being baptized by immersion in running water (mikvah) was already an accepted practice in the life of the Hebrew people.

When Jesus came to be baptized by John, it was not because He had any sin or need to be baptized; rather, it was His public identification with our humanness and sin—His entrance into the three-year ministry ending with His assuming all our sins and dying on the cross. We can see the Triune personality of God as we consider the baptism of Christ. God the Son, as a man, being baptized as He entered His public ministry; God the Father, as He spoke, "This is My beloved Son, in whom I am well pleased"; and God the Holy Spirit, descending as a dove, confirming Jesus. What a day that must have been! Although our baptism is not the same, it is indeed a wonderful day when we publicly confirm our faith in God and choose to turn away from sin and follow Him.

At or near the very spot where water divided for Joshua, five miles east of Jericho, is the location of the traditional site of Jesus' baptism. There are banana trees and palm trees along the way, reminding us that we are still in the fertile region of Jericho and its spring-fed oasis. The rushing green waters of the Jordan River took me by surprise...where are the calm waters of the Jordan I had always envisioned? Eventually, they emptied into a placid location of peaceful water which created a pool of sorts and there we were privileged to observe a beautiful baptism service take place— pilgrims from all over the world who had longed to step foot into the Jordan River were now being completely immersed in its cleansing stream.

This is a perfect time to reconsider one's life and spiritual purpose. You don't have to step into the literal waters of the Jordan in order to make your proclamation of commitment to the Lord your God. As you contemplate the serenity of a baptism in these holy waters of the Jordan, talk to God, renew your promises to Him. If you are lost or confused, please seek spiritual guidance from those you trust and may He grant you everlasting peace. If you have never committed yourself to Him, now is the time to put your feet in the Jordan and do not be afraid, for He goes before you and lovingly waits.

God waited patiently in the days of Noah while the ark was being built. In it only a few people, eight in all, were saved through water, and this water symbolizes baptism that now saves you also—not the removal of dirt from the body but the pledge of a good conscience toward God.

Peter 3:20-21, TNIV

20. GALILEE – ABUNDANT LIVING

*The people walking in darkness have seen a great
light; on those living in the land of the shadow
of death a light has dawned.*

Isaiah 9:2, NIV

Isaiah prophesied that out of *this* land would come a great Light. When we left the land of the Old Testament and headed into the land of the New Testament, I became more aware of a very obvious distinction between the two regions and considered the possibility that this contrast could be both physical and spiritual. Perhaps you will agree with me. It was very apparent that we had left the desolate, dry land of the Old Testament with its rocky wildernesses, lonely roads and emptiness. Reconciliation with God by endless attempts to be cleansed of sin was part of the past and as we entered into Galilee, we entered into the land of the ministry and miracles of the Savior.

Below is an excerpt from my journal:

"We are traveling approximately 60 miles north of Jerusalem to the Sea of Galilee, located in the northern part of the Jordan Valley, having traveled northward from the Jordan Valley near Jericho. Our journey has taken us through dry Judean hills and past former Arab 'villages,' now only ramshackled huts set in dusty enclaves. We can see the Mount of Gilead and later the Mount of Gilboa on the west and as we descend the fertile hills, the lovely Sea of

Galilee with the Golan Heights as a backdrop, come into view. There are groves of palm, eucalyptus and banana trees nearby. Our guide says that the Bible was used as a guide for agriculture and heartily tells us, 'It's a great book, so use it!' We smile and agree...how right he is!

"We stop for a view of the Syrian/Israeli frontier to the east and see snow-topped Mount Hermon straight ahead as we descend past large cotton fields to the northern end of the sea. This area includes sites of ancient Korazin which was cursed by Jesus, along with the towns of Bethsaida and Capernaum...each is in ruins to this day."

In Jesus' time, Galilee was the most northerly region of Israel. Approximately 50 miles north to south, 30 miles east to west and divided into Upper and Lower Galilee and the Sea of Galilee—it was a fruitful, productive location. After His baptism and temptation, Jesus went north to Galilee, perhaps because the flourishing towns and fertile hills were ideally suited to receive His ministry. Located along the ancient inland trade route of the Way of the Sea, the most heavily populated district included Capernaum, which lay on the northwest edge of the Sea of Galilee. It was a caravan town, a stopping place, a fishing village. In this busy setting, Jesus was able to preach and minister to the local and ever-changing mobile populace, thus reaching many. As we near Galilee, we enter into the land of miracles!

Roughly pear-shaped, the Sea of Galilee, with a 32-mile circumference, is actually a small lake approximately six miles east to west, 15 miles north to south, averaging 140 feet deep and more than 600 feet below sea level. It is the second lowest body of water on earth, topped only by the Dead Sea. It is interesting to note that one (the bromide and salt-saturated Dead Sea) holds *no life* whatsoever, while the other (the Sea of Galilee, a fresh-water lake) is *filled* with an abundance of life. In Old Testament times, it was referred to as Lake Chinnereth, Hebrew for "harp-shaped," which is the shape of the lake. Later it was also called Lake Gennesaret and the Sea of Tiberius. Because it is located in a depression in the steep hills surrounding most of the shoreline, it is subject to sudden, tumultuous storms.

More from my journal:

"Today, on a short boat ride on the lake, we can see many areas where Jesus ministered along the shores. Although we are reminded that these are only the traditional locations, it is easy to envision the man Jesus as He taught and performed so many miracles long ago, for much of the area appears now as it did then. As we drift idly across the sea, we can contemplate the amazing things that took place on this water and along its shores. An occasional fish jumps...we see gentle ripples of water...a fishing trawler is pulling a rowboat...a gull flies overhead."

The Sea of Galilee is not just another beautiful lake with nothing to offer as was the Dead Sea. Not at all, for this time there is evidence of life and bountiful harvests everywhere.

Here in Galilee, please contemplate how an often small amount of faith in our omnipotent God was exercised resulting in abundance. A perfect example is the story of the small boy, the loaves and the fishes as found in John 6:8-13. The New Testament is filled with marvelous stories of abundant life as demonstrated by the ministry of our Lord.

I would like to offer you a challenge. Has God perhaps given you a few small seeds to sow or a burden to pray for someone? Has He tugged at your heart to visit a shut-in or send someone a card? By their appearance, seeds don't offer much promise, but they are sown by the farmer in faith and in the knowledge that there *will* be a harvest. I would like to suggest that you ask the Lord what He would have you do with your "seeds" and allow Him to lead you.

> *Surely he says this for us, doesn't he? Yes, this was*
> *written for us, because when the plowman plows*
> *and the thresher threshes, they ought to do so*
> *in the hope of sharing in the harvest.*

1 Corinthians 9:10, NIV

21. COUNTING SHEEP

*"And as for you, O my flock—my people—the Lord
God says, I will judge you and separate good
from bad, sheep from goats."*

Ezekiel 34:17, TLB

As we crested the hill, our tour guide continued feeding us tidbits of historical and geographical narration. In fact, our bus driver was so totally engrossed in the dialogue, he actually took a wrong turn and had to retrace our direction. Then, without so much as a warning, the driver slowly brought the bus to a gentle stop, the guide simultaneously explaining that we had encountered a sheep crossing which was at that moment being utilized by a shepherd and his complacent flock. How exciting it was to be observing a shepherd with his sheep ambling across a modern highway in the Holy Land!

"The sheep look somewhat like goats," I wrote in my journal. As I was penning my observation, I remembered a verse (Matthew 25:32) in which Jesus said He would separate the people as a shepherd separated the sheep from the goats. In the Old Testament, there is another reference to the separation of sheep from goats. God referred to leaders as "goats," saying in Zechariah 10:3:

*"My anger burns against your 'shepherds'—your
leaders—and I will punish them—these goats."*

Judging from the appearance of these sheep, I thought this statement to be especially profound and decided to learn more about the background of this parable. I've since learned that sheep and goats were often in the same grazing and pasturing herds and that the shepherd would only separate them at shearing time. When the shepherd separated the animals of the herd, the sheep were placed to his left, the goats to his right, which also designated a place of disfavor. At shearing time, it would have been a place filled with hundreds, perhaps even thousands of bleating animals, the shepherd quickly dispersing them to his left or his right.

Reading more about this process of separation brought the Holocaust to my mind. I thought of the guards at Auschwitz and other Nazi concentration camps quickly and mercilessly assessing each innocent, suffering Jew as to his value and simply pointing—to his left—or to his right—determining their fate. I was saddened to the depths of my soul.

In his book *Night*, Holocaust survivor and author Elie Wiesel, writes about his family's arrival in Birkenau, which was the reception center for Auschwitz:

"The cherished objects we had brought with us thus far were left behind in the train, and with them, at last, our illusions. Every two yards or so an SS man held his tommy gun trained on us. Hand in hand we followed the crowd...'Men to the left! Women to the right.'

"Eight words spoken quietly, indifferently, without emotion. Eight short, simple words. Yet that was the moment when I parted from my mother. I had not had time to think, but already I felt the pressure of my father's hand: we were alone. For a part of a second I glimpsed my mother and my sister moving away to the right. Tzipora held Mother's hand. I saw them disappear into the distance; my mother was stroking my sister's fair hair, as though to protect her, while I walked on with my father and the other men. And I did not know that in that place, at that moment, I was parting from my mother and Tzipora forever. I went on walking. My father held my hand."

This was a separation made decidedly and mercilessly, designed to let live *only* those who were of use to the evil regime; all others were sent to the gas chambers. Those to the left were spared—those to the right had to die.

Jesus in His parables and David in his much-beloved 23rd Psalm, speak only of us, God's children, as sheep. We are the true followers of God and the sheep of His pasture. He knows each of us and calls us by name. We, in the world, may all look similar and appear to belong to one flock, but a time will come when those who are appointed as heirs to the Kingdom will be set apart.

I believe God's judgment will be swift and accurate. He knows His true sheep; He looks within our hearts and will make no mistake. I also believe our Father in Heaven is eager to spare each one of us a forever separation from Him. He is not merciless and He promises we will see our loved ones again in that wonderful place He has prepared for us. His eternal plan has always been that each one of us be saved from this final spiritual death and the price has already been paid with the blood of His perfect sacrificial Lamb Jesus.

Even today, in our frightening, out-of-control world, He delays Jesus' return, continually calling out the names of those who are lost or strayed. He knows them intimately, loves them unconditionally and is not willing that any be lost. May we, each one of us, do our part in helping His gathering of the flock before the final separation comes.

> *"All the nations will be gathered before him, and he will separate the people one from another as a shepherd separates the sheep from the goats."*

Matthew 25:32, NIV

22. A WALK IN GALILEE

*When a man makes a vow to the LORD or takes an
oath to obligate himself by a pledge, he must not
break his word but must do everything he said.*

Numbers 30:2, NIV

If you have ever made a serious commitment and then
not kept it, you will most likely be able to relate to this story
and perhaps read in astonishment how God made a way for
me to learn of His amazing timing and teaching process.
When I failed to keep a serious commitment some years ago,
He chose to allow me to confront my sense of guilt and bless
me at the same time! Here is how it happened:

I had been a supporter of Brother Andrew's (*God's
Smuggler*) ministry, *Open Doors*, for several years. Then, as
now, his ministry centered on the suffering Church. At the
time, the focus was on those behind the Iron Curtain and
various opportunities were provided to those of us involved
with *Open Doors* to reach out to others trapped in the
confines of Communist lands. One such prayer commitment
involved the use of a spiral-bound, table-top flip chart, each
page featuring a picture and story of individual Christian
Russians who were currently prisoners in Siberia. It was
suggested that each day we read and pray for the specific one
whose picture appeared on the chart. The following day, we
were to turn the page and pray for the next person. The flip
chart was placed on my dining room table where I could see
the face and pray each day for one of the imprisoned men.

Sadly, my zeal and prayers were not consistent and after
a few months, I fell faithless to my commitment. The same

man's face remained visible for days on end as I went about my "busy life." A pang of guilt would occasionally creep across my mind as I hurried past my dining room table endless times a day. Could I have sent a quick prayer to the Lord on his behalf during those moments? Of course! But did I? No! I thought I should be sitting on a chair or kneeling in a serious position for prayer and because of that misconception, I missed a major blessing!

Some weeks or months later, on a bright, sunny Ohio morning, I opened the Columbus Dispatch newspaper and incredulously began to read an article on the lower half of the front page. My eyes grew wide and tearful as I saw a picture of a very familiar face; it was the same picture as that of the Russian prisoner I had neglected to prayer for and whose face had looked at me during my busy times (when I didn't have time to pray for him). Above it, the words...*Russian Prisoners Freed.*

I wanted to rejoice for this freedom, but rejoicing caught in my throat! I had ignored praying for that same man on the front page of the newspaper, whose picture had stared at me from the flip chart day after day for weeks. I was immediately caught in a vice-grip of guilt! I had taken no part in his release! I could have been part of God's incredible answer through corporate prayer and yet, had turned my heart and my face away. I was so happy for him and the other prisoners, yet overwhelmed with shame. How I prayed to the Lord to forgive me for not keeping my word to continue to pray for him and the others.

I decided I would write a letter to Brother Andrew to tell him of the lesson I learned about the importance of commitment. Alas, my good intention fell victim to my "busyness" again and the letter was never written. Although I am a great saver of ephemera, I regret today that I did not save the prayer flip chart—nor did I save the newspaper article. Why I didn't, I do not know, but I think it may have had something to do with my deep feeling of guilt. By putting my head in the sand, perhaps I was attempting to deny or assuage my sense of shame.

In 1998, I went to Israel to attend the International Hospital Christian Fellowship (IHCF) Conference. Brother Andrew, IHCF Coordinator-at-Large, was to be one of the main speakers. I prayed, "Dear Lord, if it is Your will, would You arrange an opportunity for me to tell Brother Andrew my story?" I left it in God's hands, feeling certain He would work out the details.

A few days later, we prepared for an all-day tour of Jericho and the Dead Sea area. As we queued up for the morning handouts of bottled water and snacks, Brother Andrew, who was in front of me in the line, turned and greeted me. After a few minutes of conversation, I mentioned my hope for an opportunity to tell him the story regarding his ministry and the prisoner. He replied, "I would love to hear it—perhaps we can talk on the bus during one of our tours."

This didn't happen, however. The tour continued and a week later, we were staying at a kibbutz in Galilee, each with his own personal cottage (plus one roommate). It was but a short walk past other cottages to the shore of the Sea of Galilee. I could not believe I was there on the very shores where Jesus had sat and talked with His followers.

One afternoon, while my roommate was resting, I walked to the shore planning to do some journaling. Along the way, I saw Brother Andrew standing on the sidewalk in front of his modest cottage. Maybe today, I thought, I will have my chance to tell him about the Russian prisoner. However, another gentleman came along and the two of them began a conversation. I was content, knowing it was "their time to meet."

About an hour later, I stopped writing and headed back toward my cottage. I again saw Brother Andrew in front of his. We greeted each other and this time, as if he was being guided, he walked toward me and said hello a second time. I mentioned that I had not yet had the opportunity to tell him the astounding way that I had learned about the freed Russian prisoners.

He quickly replied, "Well, why not now? Do you want to take a walk? Which way would you like to go?"

I had two choices: first, we could turn around and walk toward the Sea of Galilee, or second, we could walk forward along a dirt road leading toward the distant mountains. I was astonished by his offer to take the time to talk to me and decision-making was not something I wanted to ponder. I chose to walk along the dusty road in Galilee and in that incredible setting, God arranged the time for me to tell Brother Andrew my story, along with the valuable lesson I had learned regarding the importance of keeping a commitment.

God's allowance for me to walk and talk with one of His obedient servants was beyond my comprehension. It was in His perfect way and in His perfect timing for I never expected to be relating the experience to Brother Andrew himself while walking along a dirt road in Galilee. I did not understand then, nor do I today except that more than 20 years later, I am now writing about this experience and sharing it with you.

Do you want to walk where Jesus walked? You can...take the dusty road of life, for it surely exists...and take along your own story. Share it with someone. God will bless you and the listener in a most amazing way and remember, if you have made a pledge of commitment to the Lord, keep your promise, keep your word. He is waiting to bless you. My blessing is in the writing of this story, with its example from my own life. I pray that it challenges you to a stronger desire to keep your commitments to our God who keeps His every promise.

> *The Lord is not slow in keeping his promise, as some*
> *understand slowness. He is patient with you, not*
> *wanting anyone to perish, but everyone to come*
> *to repentance.*

2 Peter 3:9, NIV

23. THE BLESSED MAKEOVER

The Lord called me before my birth. From within the womb he called me by name.

Isaiah 49:1, TLB

It was a perfect day to walk along the shore at the Sea of Galilee and contemplate the Lord. So many of the wonderful stories of Jesus' ministry had taken place right here along its coastline and upon its waters. I thought of Jesus calming the storm and walking on the water, nets straining to an overwhelming catch of fish, the feeding of the five thousand and the appearance of Christ to His followers after His resurrection. (Read all of Matthew, chapter 21 for Jesus' visit with the disciples after His resurrection.)

The scene was relaxing as I walked alone beneath the canopy of a brilliant blue sky. A lively brisk breeze was kicking up some choppy waves and a few colorful sailboats plied the water, but I dismissed them in favor of thoughts of the rugged, hand-hewn fishing boats of long ago. The landscape in the distance reminded me very much of the California hillsides. Closer to shore, eucalyptus and palm trees blowing in the wind provided shade and a pleasant cooling to my skin. A solitary hoopoe bird tiptoed along in the grass, seeking a tasty morsel for its noonday meal.

As I wandered along, I asked the Man who once walked these shores, "Am I doing all You have planned for me, Lord? Will I be an *overcomer* in these last days before You return? I am so grateful to be here in the very land where You spent

Your earthly life and taught us about the Father. I long to follow You and be with You forever, Jesus."

A whisper in the breeze...

"Look down, Carol. What do you see?"

I glanced down at the shoreline where small wet stones and rocks glistened as the foamy surf ebbed and flowed upon them and what I noticed beneath my feet were numerous white stones scattered among the others. Unexpectedly, I remembered some words of Scripture from Revelation used in a teaching earlier that week which included the promise of a new name written on a white stone for those who overcome this world.

I began thinking about my new name—I wonder what it will be, I mused. I thought of the verses I had read that tells us how individually God thinks about us. He even has our names engraved on the palms of His hands!

See, I have engraved you on the palms of my hands.

Isaiah 49:16, NIV

Especially appealing is the fact that He has pet names for each of us, just as He does for the billions upon billions of stars in the universe.

He determines the number of the stars
and calls them each by name.

Psalm 147:4, NIV

He also calls His sheep by name.

The watchman opens the gate for him, and the sheep listen
to his voice. He calls his own sheep by name and leads
them out.

John 10:3, NIV

These are such endearing words concerning the Father's love and thoughts regarding us.

They blessed me so much as I contemplated my given name— Carol. I shared my inner thoughts with Him saying, "I've read that

Carol means 'song of joy,' but Lord, so often over the years, I have not felt joy, but sorrow instead."

I sensed His arm across my shoulder, and in my spirit, there were loving words reminding me *He* is my joy and I was at peace once again.

Out of the blue, an enticing thought entered my mind, so I stooped down and began picking up the white stones until I had enough for each member of my family. I already knew what I would do with them. I took them back home and before I gave them away, I wrote individual names along with the scripture verse from Revelation 2:17 on each one. The stones became meaningful little souvenirs—each of my loved ones received their earthly name written on a white stone plucked from the shores of the Sea of Galilee and inscribed with the scripture to remind them that Jesus Himself will give them a new name one day.

Over the years, the thought of my new name continued to intrigue me. During an emotional crisis in my life when I was hospitalized in a Christian treatment center, my favorite song titled *I Will Give You a New Name*, was a great encouragement to me. The words reminded me not only of that promise once again, but also that I *must* be an overcomer, no matter the circumstances.

A little research information regarding the white stones may interest you also. These stones or tokens were of great significance during Roman times. Often they were given to victorious Roman soldiers and provided them access to everything; events, lodging— even banquets! The verse in Revelation would have had a deep meaning to the early Christians living under Roman rule as they contemplated the stone promised for each one who overcomes— entrance to the wedding banquet of the Lamb and His Holy Bride, the Church.

And the angel said to me, "Write this: Blessed are those who are invited to the wedding feast of the Lamb."

Revelation 19:9, NLT

As you think about these things, picture yourself at the wedding feast. Just think! We who overcome shall each be there and we shall have our new names!

To him who overcomes, I will give some of the hidden manna. I will also give him a white stone with a new name written on it, known only to him who receives it.

Revelation 2:17, NIV

24. "GONE FISHING"

Whether you turn to the right or to the left, your
ears will hear a voice behind you, saying,
"This is the way; walk in it."

Isaiah 30:21, NIV

Near the lake, cool evening breezes fanned the flickering campfire just enough to briefly brighten the faces of the three men crouched around it. The once gentle lapping of the waves against the pebbled shore had suddenly increased in strength and frequency, causing the men to comment on their decision to come ashore.

"Storm's definitely coming," the long-bearded one said. "We need to be putting our gear away after we eat. There will be no fishing on the lake tonight."

"You're right, Thaddeus," said the man next to him. "We've been in storms on this lake before. I'm just glad it blew in before we were too far out on the water."

The group had taken their boat out at dusk, planning to fish all night. However, the rise of the wind and the ever-darkening evening clouds changed their plans. Returning to shore, they moored the boat, made a small wood fire and prepared to broil the few fish they had caught. Supper would be meager this evening, with only a few pieces of bread to add to their meal.

All of the men lived in a small village on the northwest side of the lake. Friends since childhood, each was familiar with the danger of going out on the lake if the weather warned otherwise, and although fishing was their livelihood, they knew when it was wise to remain on shore.

The crickets' chirping call, along with the hoarse quacks of the pelicans and the low whistle-like sound of the grebes added to the wild splashing sound of the waves, providing a background of sorts as they ate their dinner.

"It's the strangest thing," Thaddeus said, "the way those two left town yesterday."

The other men nodded in agreement, their mouths busy with fish and bread.

"I imagine everyone in town has heard about it by now. You have to wonder what in the world would make two busy fishermen take off like that...and in the middle of the day! I heard they didn't even say goodbye to their families."

The shortest of the group, Daniel, stood up, stretched his arms and walked toward the shore. In a pensive tone, he said, "There was something about that fellow who came walking by the boats yesterday. I saw him. He walked over to Simon and Andrew while they were tending to their nets and stood there beside their boat, gesturing first toward the lake and then to their nets. Those two brothers didn't turn their eyes away from Him the whole time He was talking to them. Whatever He said must have been very important because they put down the nets, got out of the boat and walked off down the road with Him. I heard He's from over the hills in Nazareth...a carpenter, I think. It's strange that He walked all the way to Capernaum just to talk to people along the lake. I wonder what He wanted with those men. Maybe He asked them to teach Him how to fish. I watched them leave together. They hadn't walked very far before Andrew came running back to their boat. He put a sign on it—a message for their father, I've been told. Yet that's another strange thing...the sign only had two words on it... "GONE FISHING." For some reason, I'm wishing I had joined them."

> *"Come, follow me," Jesus said, "and I*
> *will make you fishers of men."*
>
> Matthew 4:19, NIV

You have heard His voice. He has called each of us to a purpose. Ask Him today what it is He requires of you and rest assured; you will be equipped fully for the task.

25. DESOLATE CITIES

*Then they will take up a lament concerning you and
say to you: "How you are destroyed, O city
of renown, peopled by men of the sea!"*

Ezekiel 26:17, NIV

Leaving Capernaum prompted a feeling of loneliness
within me. It had been the center of Jesus' earthly ministry
and yet it was empty—in fact, in ruins. It didn't have to be
this way, you know, but as we read in Matthew 11:21-24, it is
one of three cities which Jesus cursed because of its citizens'
refusal to repent of their sins and disbelief in His divinity.

*Then Jesus began to denounce the cities in which
most of his miracles had been performed, because
they did not repent. "Woe to you, Korazin! Woe to
you, Bethsaida! If the miracles that were performed
in you had been performed in Tyre and Sidon, they
would have repented long ago in sackcloth and
ashes. But I tell you, it will be more bearable
for Tyre and Sidon on the day of judgment
than for you* [Ezekiel 26:19, tells of Tyre's
condemnation]. *And you, Capernaum,
will you be lifted up to the skies? No,
you will go down to the depths. If
the miracles that were performed
in you had been performed in
Sodom, it would have remained
to this day. But I tell you that
it will be more bearable for
Sodom on the day of
judgment than for you."*

Matthew 11:20-24, NIV

I wondered why Jesus ever chose to settle here, knowing as only He would, the outcome. I was contemplating the fact that if I knew I would not be accepted in a spot before I even located my ministry there, I would have chosen a more receptive region, rather than set myself up for failure. Not so Jesus, for in His wisdom and for His purposes, Capernaum and its surrounding fishing villages were chosen not only to be the center of His ministry (as Capernaum was), but also to be the setting for the majority of His astonishing miracles. Wonders upon wonders occurred in this region: great indisputable evidence of His supernatural authority over nature such as calming the tempestuous winds and walking upon, even speaking to, an obedient sea; His healing command over all manner of disease and even death; His spectacular provision of abundance, such as the feeding of the 5,000.

Why and *how* could they have disbelieved in Him? How it must have saddened His heart toward His creation (man) when even after seeing His miracles, they still rejected Him, refusing to repent of their sinful ways and follow Him.

About two and a half miles north of the remains of Capernaum lie black basalt reminders of what once was Chorazin (Korazin), another of the cursed cities. As you climb the elevation, you can see where each of the cities once were, for they sat in a triangular formation just a few miles from one another.

Approximately three miles east of Capernaum, close to the coastline of the Sea of Galilee had been the city of Bethsaida, hometown of Peter, Andrew and Philip and quite possibly the site of the feeding of the 5,000. We understand from the Scriptures how well-known Jesus was and how the multitudes sought Him out as they heard of His miracles. There was only one means of communication then—word of mouth. The region must have been buzzing with excitement and amazement at the incredulous stories spread among the local inhabitants. How is it then that this same population would be so unbelieving as to warrant His pronouncement of destruction? It is difficult to understand, but as I contemplate this fact, I am prompted to consider how many times Jesus has heard my pleas, often answering them in miraculous ways and yet my faith often flounders. When I sense the seed of doubt trying to germinate and tangle my thinking, distracting me from my true belief, I am reminded of the denizens of these now-desolate cities. Am I like one of those? True, I have not physically seen Jesus, but I have, in all probability, been blessed by His divine intervention in my life more times than any one person who flocked to see and listen to Him 2,000 years ago. My faith cannot depend upon a visual encounter, for it is faith in that which is not seen that honors God.

Thank you, Lord, for entrusting this wondrous relationship to me. Thank you for your enabling power to sustain me when I weaken and question my faith. May I ever honor you for all you have done for me.

> *...blessed are those who have not seen and*
> *yet have believed.*
>
> John 20:29, NIV

26. THE VALLEY OF THE DOVES

*Even though I walk through the valley of the shadow
of death, I will fear no evil; for you are with me.*

Psalm 23:4, NIV

We reluctantly left the region of the three cities, now in ruins and headed west toward Cana and Nazareth. It was heartrending to me that these three cities did not have to receive this curse; the people had a choice to believe in the One who had performed so many miracles in their midst, but their decision was to deny Him. They lived in the land prophesied by Isaiah; they saw the light and yet they denied Him.

As we rode toward the mountains of Galilee, we were told that Jesus often walked along this way from Nazareth and Cana to Capernaum, as it was a frequently used route.

"We are now entering the Valley of the Doves," bellowed the tour guide, his voice rising above the chatter and hymn singing of the pilgrims on the bus.

As the bus bumped along, I gave the name of the region some serious consideration. Perhaps doves were hunted and slated for sacrifice at the Temple in Jerusalem...that would be a good reason to name this area the Valley of the Doves. The name sounded so pure and innocent, peaceful and calm. However, our guide's fastidious entertaining rendering of historical and geographical facts and legends transformed my mental visualization of idyllic green pastures in valleys dotted with multi-colored meadow flowers and flocks of peaceful doves soaring the sky above. His narrative quickly showed that my thoughts were far from realistic regarding this rough and rugged terrain.

From the shores of the lake at Capernaum, one can see the lofty landmark of Mount Arbel rising more than 800 feet above sea level. As we entered the area shadowed by this towering plateau, upon which rest rocky remnants of long-expired volcanoes, the pastoral scene in my mind turned more ominous. We were told that the "rift" in the land at the base of Mount Arbel is what is actually known as the Valley of the Doves and it was, in the time of Jesus, known as a treacherous and foreboding pathway with steep, rugged cliffs on either side. The valley was a natural, but risky portion of an access route to the area of the Sea of Galilee from inland towns and villages and was actually a wadi (a channel or valley through which water flows during the heavy rainy season).

I tried to imagine a four-day walking journey from Nazareth to Capernaum and on the third day of travel, entering such a valley where nighttime is black, isolating and cold, rocky cliffs obscure the nightlight of the heavens. I wondered what wild creatures might have inhabited the caves or padded silently along the rocky heights searching the darkness for prey. In the summer season, the daytime heat soared to unbearable limits and during winter, the same deep valley functioned more as a wind tunnel allowing the superheated winds coursing in from the west to become increasingly powerful. Thus, the severe harsh winds often swooshed down upon the shallow Sea of Galilee, yielding the sudden and extreme storms of which we have read in the gospels.

It has been suggested that this valley could be the one referred to in Psalm 23 as the "valley of the shadow of death" and with good reason. Historically, it has been the site of many wars where horrible atrocities committed by invading conquerors have occurred.

I wondered, could it be this very spot? Even if it is not, for me, the placid-sounding Valley of the Doves will always serve as a visual reminder as I contemplate any valley of my life. The valley of the shadow of death can be anywhere, anytime—when I am sick, when I am lonely or destitute, when I am depressed beyond my ability to help myself. When the world around me trembles, I will visualize the Valley of the Doves and remember as the beloved Psalm tells me—"I will fear no evil."

> *Leaving Nazareth, he went and lived in Capernaum, which was by the lake in the area of Zebulun and Naphtali.*

Matthew 4:13, NIV

27. NO CHILD IN NAZARETH

Then I will remove my hand and you will see my back; but my face must not be seen.

Exodus 33:23, NIV

As the dusty tour bus entered the steep, hilly city of Nazareth, my heartbeat increased with anticipation. I was planning to take the perfect picture of the first little boy I saw—it would be a great jumpstart for me if I later decided to write a story about this part of the journey through the Holy Land. What more could I ask for than a small boy walking along a street in Jesus' childhood hometown?

The bus ambled on, at times gasping its way up streets which had somehow become more like inclines. It was incredibly hot! Eventually, we arrived at our destination, the Nazareth Hospital which was built in 1861 and now operated by the Edinborough Medical Missionary Society. As a Christian medical group, we certainly appreciated the tour and were quite impressed with the various departments noting the cleanliness, organization and up-to-date equipment available to the citizens of Nazareth.

Soon it was time to leave our friendly hospital guides and climb the steep street to where the bus was parked, our chests heaving with the effort. I resumed scanning the streets and alleyways as the bus traversed the city, but to my dismay, I saw not one little boy to photograph and before long, we were on the outskirts of the city.

I began to ponder my reason for searching the empty streets in hopes of sighting a small boy in Nazareth. Did I really expect to find someone who would fit my vision of the child Jesus? Are there any artists' renderings of Jesus drawn from life? The answer, of course, is no. I'm so glad I didn't see a child in Nazareth to photograph, for just as there are no images of God, I do believe the Lord does not desire us to find substitutes of any sort. Our relationship with Him is totally dependent on faith in what we cannot see. Jesus, knowing full well our human nature, mentioned that to His disciples after His resurrection when He visited with them.

> *Then Jesus told him, "Because you have seen me,*
> *you have believed; blessed are those who have*
> *not seen and yet have believed."*

John 20:29, NIV

A short while later, as we were leaving Nazareth, the guide pointed out a location to our left saying this was the spot where the townspeople attempted to toss Jesus over the cliff. The visual picture, with Mount Tabor only a few miles away, pierced my heart. I thought of Him denounced and ridiculed in His own hometown. Gone was my idea of a little boy in Nazareth to photograph; replacing it was the thought of His rejection, of His being forced to the outskirts of the city by an angry mob. I wonder now—was this a portent of the final rejection yet to come? Scripture points out that He walked away through the crowd and left them [for it was not yet His time to die].

> *All the people in the synagogue were furious when they*
> *heard this. They got up, drove him out of the town,*
> *and took him to the brow of the hill on which the*
> *town was built, in order to throw him down the*
> *cliff. But he walked right through the crowd*
> *and went on his way.*

Luke 4:28-30, NIV

As you contemplate the rejection the young man Jesus received by the residents of His hometown, maybe you can remember a time (or times) when you were hurt or rebuffed by friends or family. Perhaps it felt as though you were the only one who has ever felt such a deep sense of dismissal and loneliness. Remember that Jesus the man endured everything here on earth that we must and understands our pain and sorrow in all circumstances. Keep your eyes on Jesus whom we have not seen and in whom we yet believe for the rewards are great.

So we fix our eyes not on what is seen, but on what is unseen. For what is seen is temporary, but what is unseen is eternal.

2 Corinthians 4:18, NIV

28. MOUNT TABOR

*You created north and south. Mount Tabor and
Mount Hermon praise your name.*

Psalm 89:12, NLT

About ten miles southwest of the Sea of Galilee and a few miles south of Nazareth, rising more than 1,000 feet from the Jezreel Valley, is a rather nondescript round-topped mountain. The mountain doesn't appear to have any peculiarities other than its high dome shape and the fact that from a few miles distance it seems to be just sitting there all alone. In any other environment I suppose most people wouldn't give it more than a passing glance, but we had just left Nazareth and our guide had pointed it out to us saying, "There in the distance is Mount Tabor, the traditional site of the transfiguration of Jesus."

That statement changed everything! Instead of just being a run-of-the-mill hill, it suddenly represented the location of perhaps the most awesome occurrence in the life of Jesus up to this point. Knowing that soon He would be on the tree of His sacrifice for all mankind, He also understood that virtually no one comprehended who He was and why He had come to earth. Jesus had told His followers and many others who He was and even though He had fulfilled so many of the long-awaited prophecies, they just didn't understand. I suppose that caused a searing in His heart to know that the very ones who had spent the last three years at His side, who had seen Him command the wind and the sea, who had marveled when He healed all manner of disease and infirmities still did not recognize Him as the Messiah. He knew what lay ahead for Him in His beloved city of Jerusalem, and that the same three disciples He invited to climb this mountain with Him that day would also deny Him when He was at the point of death.

Nevertheless, He asked Peter, James and John to accompany Him as He climbed Mount Tabor to pray. There the astounding transfiguration of Jesus occurred as the mortal men observed a phenomenon that surely was both startling and bewildering. Almost before they could think, they were confronted with an astonishing vision of the glorified Jesus.

As he was praying, the appearance of his face changed, and his clothes became as bright as a flash of lightning.

Luke 9:29, NIV

Then, without warning, two others were in attendance with Jesus. Hadn't the four of them just climbed this mountain...Jesus, Peter, James and John?

Two men, Moses and Elijah, appeared in glorious splendor, talking with Jesus. They spoke about his departure, which he was about to bring to fulfillment at Jerusalem.

Luke 9:30-31, NIV

I can't imagine the fear and amazement Peter, James and John must have felt, but I wonder what they might have said, if anything. At a time like this, mere words could not have been sufficient. Mark 9:5 tells us that Peter suggested putting up some shelters for the three heavenly men, but he goes on to say in verse 7 that Peter was interrupted by a voice coming from a cloud which enveloped them.

While he was still speaking, a bright cloud enveloped them, and a voice from the cloud said, "This is my Son, whom I love; with him I am well pleased. Listen to him!"

Matthew 17:5, NIV

This experience had to have been indescribable. How can humans ever explain the splendor and magnificence of God?

The disciples kept this to themselves, and told no one at
that time what they had seen.

Luke 9:36, NIV

We all are speechless before Him; words are not sufficient. The Bible uses majestic descriptions of His creation to tell of His glory and it is good to contemplate them.

You are resplendent with light, more majestic than
mountains rich with game.

Psalm 76:4, NIV

The heavens declare the glory of God; the skies proclaim
the work of his hands. Day after day they pour forth
speech; night after night they display knowledge. There is
no speech or language where their voice is not heard.

Psalm 19:1-3, NIV

As we descend Mount Tabor, having had a glimpse of the glory bestowed upon Jesus so soon before His death, let us reflect on His honor, His magnificence and His splendor! Praise Him for who He is in all of creation and for who He is in your own life. Be enveloped in the cloud of His majesty and thank Him for His gift of eternal life for one day you *shall* behold Him in all His glory, just as these three friends did!

We did not follow cleverly invented stories when we told
you about the power and coming of our Lord Jesus
Christ, but we were eyewitnesses of his majesty.
For he received honor and glory from God the
Father when the voice came to him from the
Majestic Glory, saying, "This is my Son,
whom I love; with him I am well pleased."
We ourselves heard this voice that came
from heaven when we were with him
on the sacred mountain.

2 Peter 1:16-18, NIV

29. MEGIDDO

*And I will bring the blind by a way that they knew
not; I will lead them in paths that they have not
known: I will make darkness light before them,
and crooked things straight. These things
will I do unto them, and not forsake them.*

Isaiah 42:16, KJV

On our way to Megiddo, we overlooked the expansive, beautiful Jezreel Valley, our bus careening on hairpin curves. We could see Mount Tabor (traditional site of Jesus' Transfiguration) to our left with the Jezreel Valley in the foreground; Mount Gilboa, also to our left, was where King Saul died. Soon we entered the Valley of Armageddon spoken of in the Bible and my camera could scarcely capture the spectacular view of this piece of land where the final battle would take place—the western aspect of the valley was expansive and very beautiful!

The bus was parked and we climbed up to Tel Megiddo overlooking the New Testament site of Armageddon and walked through ruins dating from the time of King Solomon and beyond. For thousands of years, Megiddo held a most strategic military location at the head of a mountain pass, guarding entrance or exit to the Way of the Sea, the vital overland coastal route to the Mediterranean Sea. The city belonged to the Canaanites in 1500 BC. Many years later, King Solomon fortified the city, perhaps to protect the Temple in Jerusalem, the heart of Israel only 70 miles south. Archeologists have unearthed more than 30 levels of civilization dating back to at least 6,000 years BC. The commanding view of the Jezreel Valley was overwhelming and as we walked along the remnants of prior civilizations, I stopped to take a picture of a stone manger, used perhaps by the horses belonging to King Solomon who used this location as a chariot city stabling many horses.

The most fascinating and perhaps what Megiddo is most famous for is the unbelievable tunnel built in 950 BC that leads from within the city to its water source, a spring which lays outside the city. The tunnel, completely straight, was chiseled and hammered into being by the hands of men starting at both ends and when they met, they were only one foot apart from each other. Our tour included walking the stone paths of antiquity as we descended the steps of King Ahab's 120-foot-deep shaft and traversed the tunnel where marks can still be seen on the rocks. Our vision enhanced by electricity, we reached the ancient spring and climbed the exit steps into the sunlight once again, but we were reminded by our guide that in the days of its use, there was no walkway or lighting and all water was collected by the women of the city in total darkness. The tunnel, nearly 220 feet long, is considered one of the greatest engineering feats of all time and is well worth investigating further by way of the internet and local library.

It would not have been easy to go through a tunnel in utter darkness, especially one of this length, I thought. Dangerous enough would have been the steps leading down the shaft to the tunnel—the women very easily could have tripped or missed a step as they descended. Accidents that could lead to an instant dark and cold eternal grave were most likely commonplace.

Our life without Christ can be likened to walking into the depths of a pitch-black tunnel. Without light, the way is treacherous, lonely and we can trip over unknown obstacles that can cause our physical death much like walking without the Light can lead to spiritual death. I am so grateful that God has promised to show us the way by sending to us the Light of the world, aren't you? Let us each pray that we can learn more of Jesus and follow the path He has set for us.

I have come into the world as a light, so that no one who believes in me should stay in darkness.

John 12:46, NIV

30. MANGER IN MEGIDDO

*And I will pour out on the house of David and the
inhabitants of Jerusalem a spirit of grace and
supplication. They will look on me, the one they
have pierced, and they will mourn for him as one
mourns for an only child, and grieve bitterly for
him as one grieves for a firstborn son. On that
day the weeping in Jerusalem will be great,
like the weeping of Hadad Rimmon in
the plain of Megiddo.*

Zechariah 12:10-11, NIV

Along the ancient route to the sea (Via Maris) lie the
ruins of Megiddo, once the most important city in the Jezreel
Valley. Strategically located at the entrance to a narrow
pass leading to the coastal plains of Israel, it dates back to
over 3,000 years BC as a large and prosperous city, well-
fortified and amply supplied with water.

The mound at Megiddo was massive and from its
summit, one could barely grasp the immensity of the Jezreel
Valley it overlooked. As my eyes swept across this beautiful
vista, I breathed in a quick gasp and attempted to visualize
the many bloody battles of antiquity that had taken place on
this very spot. Our Israeli guide proudly recounted its
history—"Layers of 21 cities dating back as far as 3,000
BC"..."King Solomon had one of three chariot cities built
here"..."mangers which are remnants of King Ahab's stables
are here."

At the mention of chariots, horse stables and mangers,
my mind wandered back to the crudely-carved block of stone
we had just passed. The newborn baby Jesus was placed in

a manger! Did it look like *this*? I thought of His delicate skin, fragile as the inner petal of a rosebud being placed on a rough-hewn slab of rock such as this! Somehow, I wanted to dismiss this unpleasant thought, but then I remembered the swaddling clothes mentioned in the Scriptures. They would have protected His baby skin, wouldn't they? Besides, Mary used the hay which lay in the manger for cattle feed as a type of mattress for Him. Not the down-filled cloud of softness we would like to think of as a sleeping spot for our Creator, but nevertheless, it was the mattress of His heavenly Father's choosing.

Only a few days before, we had visited Bethlehem. There we had been informed that the "stable" in which He was born was most likely a cave in the hillside. This possibility was still very fresh in my mind as we walked amidst the ruins of ancient Megiddo.

We often speak of His lowly beginnings, His humble lifestyle and yet our minds and songs have created a picturesque and rather storybook idea of His birth. In reality, giving birth to the King of Kings in a cave meant for livestock, and having no bed in which to place their newborn son must have been extremely difficult for the parents. After all, they knew He was the Messiah, the Promised One. Placing Him in what was simply a trough cut in the rocky wall of a cave may also have anguished the chosen parents, for they were just like us and would have wanted the best for their infant Son.

He was wrapped in swaddling clothes, as was the custom of the time. These were strips of material, woven finely or not, in accordance with the parents' wealth. Shepherds, heeding the sign from the angels, would most likely have begun their search not just for a baby in swaddling clothes, but for one lying in a livestock feeding trough in one of the cold damp caves surrounding Bethlehem.

I reflected on our recent visit to the Garden Tomb in Jerusalem, which is viewed as a possible site of our Lord's burial. Was it not also in a cave? Was there not also a slab of stone on which His precious body lay? It was not even His own, but rather a borrowed resting spot in a family tomb with slabs perhaps hewn from the walls of the cave on which to place the bodies of the deceased.

According to the gospels, His body was wrapped in a long linen cloth and placed in the tomb of Joseph of Arimathea. Three days later, the empty tomb contained only the neatly folded burial cloths of Jesus. His earthly ministry ended as it began—in a cave meant for others, on a slab of stone as a resting place. He never did have a bed of His own, did He?

The God of Heaven and Creator of all gave up His place in glory for the likes of me! I am so unworthy of this kind of love; I can hardly comprehend it. Thank you, dear baby Jesus—thank you, precious dying Savior—and praise You, Lord of all creation—for Your gift of love and sacrifice for each of us. I offer myself to You today and ask that You use me to share Your love with others. I long for Your return!

"In my Father's house are many rooms; if it were not so,
I would have told you. I am going there to
prepare a place for you."

John 14:2, NIV

31. HE CARRIED THE WOOD

Then God said, "Take your son, your only son,
Isaac, whom you love, and go to the region
of Moriah. Sacrifice him there as a burnt
offering on one of the mountains I will
tell you about."

Genesis 22:2, NIV

What does it do to a father's heart when the sacrifice of his beloved son is asked of him? How deep is the cut? How searing the pain? A more severe test of faith cannot be found than that which was required of Abraham by the God of Heaven. How closely must he have walked and talked with God to be able to say yes to this command. Please take a moment to contemplate the painful choice Abraham made by obeying God.

The three-day journey from Beer-sheba to the land of Moriah must have been one of agony for Abraham. He had no idea that one day he would be referred to as the "father of the faith." He only knew love and obedience to his Father in Heaven. His complete devotion to God remains an enigma. Many ask how he could have remained faithful to God when the ultimate was required of him—the horrible bloodletting sacrifice upon a blazing pyre, of his long-awaited son Isaac.

Each step of the 60-mile journey must have felt like the pounding of a nail into his skull; each huff of breath a reminder of the brief life his son would have and of Isaac's soon-to-be final gasps of air in the consuming fire which awaited him.

Each moment with his son must have been cherished, yet blurred by the vision of what he must do when they reached the site where obedience to his sovereign God would usurp his deep love for his young son. There would be no one else to plunge the knife—no one present to comfort his boy.

On the third day of the journey, leaving the two accompanying servants behind, Abraham and his son continued the remainder of the long trip together. They stopped at the base of the hill known as Mount Moriah. There a dramatic change took place. Father Abraham, knowing what lay ahead for each of them, placed the wood for the fire upon young Isaac's shoulders; Abraham carried the knife and flint with which to start the fire. Father and son began climbing to the spot on Mount Moriah that God had shown Abraham, Isaac unknowingly carrying the wood upon which he would be sacrificed while his father bore his own burden of grief in stunning silence.

At the precise moment that Abraham raised his knife to pierce his son's heart, God spoke, telling him to lay down his knife. He had passed the ultimate test of faith. A substitution ram was provided by the Lord to be sacrificed in place of Isaac. Some may wonder at God's plan for Abraham and Isaac that fateful day, but God's plan for man, of which this was a part, had already been set in place before the beginning of time.

Carrying his own cross, he went out to the place of the Skull (which in Aramaic is called Golgotha).

John 19:17, NIV

More than 2,000 years later, God's own Son would be led up this same hill to be crucified. He, too, would carry the wood upon His back as He climbed Mount Moriah to His Golgotha. This time there would be no substitution. The Lamb of God, perfect and without blemish, would be sacrificed. God would not intervene as He did on behalf of Isaac. Instead, filled with unfathomable grief, He gave the life and the life's blood of His only Son Jesus in order that His divine purpose for our salvation would be fulfilled. Not only the wood, but also the sins of the world lay upon the macerated flesh of our Savior and each agonizing step was soon echoed by the pounding of cruel nails into His hands and feet. God could have intervened, but He did not. His eternal love and compassion for us is beyond our comprehension. Read the words that follow and thank God for His perfect expression of love, the sacrifice of His only Son Jesus.

*He who did not spare His own Son, but gave Him up
for us all—how will He not also, along with Him,
graciously give us all things?*

Romans 8:32, NIV

32. GOING UP TO JERUSALEM

Three times a year all your men must appear before
the LORD your God at the place he will choose: at
the Feast of Unleavened Bread, the Feast of Weeks
and the Feast of Tabernacles.

Deuteronomy 16:16, NIV

As pilgrims in the Holy Land, it is fitting I believe, to conclude our journey where it started—in the city of Jerusalem.

God's mandate to the Hebrew males, as in the Scripture above, meant waiting and saving for the journey, perhaps for many long years, traveling scores of miles, usually by foot and often bringing along the family. Although the trip was primarily for religious purposes, what could be more exciting than a journey to the Holy City of God, where one could see the Temple and mingle with fellow travelers and worshippers?

The thought of this trip reminds me of the excitement that leads up to state or county fairs in today's world. We plan in advance when we will be going, save our vacation days and money and bring food in our vehicles, perhaps in an effort to save money. Upon arrival, if one has a camper or RV, the first thing to do is seek out a parking area and get settled before suppertime. The kids have been singing and talking non-stop the entire trip and now their excitement is almost beyond control. Knowing other friends and family will most likely be among the throngs of people means everyone will be keeping a lookout for someone they know or agreed to meet up with during pre-trip plans.

It was probably a lot like this in long ago Israel and Jerusalem. Picture the travelers, laughing and talking as they wend their way along well-worn roads and paths leading to the Holy City. The kids most likely would have been filled to overflowing with excitement, incessantly chattering and giggling, running back and forth among the crowds looking for friends or perhaps cousins. The parents would probably have had quite a time keeping them in tow and trying to keep them from getting lost. (Remember the story of 12-year-old Jesus who journeyed from Nazareth with his family only to be discovered to be missing on the return trip.)

Jerusalem's population usually quadrupled during times of pilgrimages and this would have provided great, if only temporary, economical stimulation. Expenses would have included the cost of food, lodging, sacrificial animals and a tithe to the Temple. Pilgrims were also expected to spend one tenth of their annual income (after taxes) within Jerusalem—this was called the "second tithe." The need for lodging increased so much during festivals that many of the travelers pitched tents outside the city or stayed in private homes in villages close by, such as Bethphage or Bethany on the eastern side of the Mount of Olives.

Since the city was also controlled by the Romans, soldiers would have been stationed throughout the city and its surroundings because of the possibility of problems due to overcrowding and enthusiastic festival-goers.

The following, quoted from *The Source* by James Michener, provides a unique insight into the experience of going "up to Jerusalem" as seen from the eyes of the fictional character Rimmon, who is traveling with his mother Gomer to the fall festival.

"The journey up to Jerusalem in that hot month of Ethanim was, as Yahweh had intended, an experience that Rimmon would never forget, although while undergoing it he perceived it as a physical adventure rather than as a spiritual ascent. It was a distance of more than ninety miles over difficult and wearing terrain, to be finished in the hot time of autumn, so that the journey occupied eight days.

"Mother and son left the zigzag gate at dawn, a tall pair dressed in the cheapest clothes, shod in heavy sandals and carrying staves. On their backs, they carried a little food, in their purses a few pieces of silver, but Rimmon had with him an additional item that would prove of considerable value: lengths of cord with which to build his booth on the slopes leading up to Jerusalem's walls.

"In the first hours they climbed without actually seeing the noble city, but they were assured that they were on the right path by the hundreds of other pilgrims streaming in from outlying regions to celebrate in Jerusalem the high holy days which marked the beginning of each new year.

"Gomer and her son were struggling up the last steep, rocky path, surrounded by barren hills and deep wadis, when they heard ahead of them the joyful chant of people singing the traditional songs of the ascent:

> "I rejoiced when they said unto me:
> 'Let us go into the house of the Yahweh.'
> Our feet are standing within your gates, O Jerusalem…
> Whither the tribes go up, even the tribes of Yahweh."

As we prepare to enter the city chosen by God as His residence, we will have ample time to ponder His great gift of sacrifice for us. May we never forget our journey to His holy hill, knowing that our arrival is but a foretaste of what lies ahead for the faithful. One day, we will see the glorious New Jerusalem, spoken of by John in the book of Revelation:

> *I saw the Holy City, the new Jerusalem, coming down out*
> *of heaven from God, prepared as a bride beautifully*
> *dressed for her husband.*

Revelation 21:2, NIV

33. ENTER THE KING

The glory of the LORD went up from within the city
and stopped above the mountain east of it.

Ezekiel 11:23, NIV

It had been a long and tiring walk from the oasis city of Jericho to the southeastern slopes of the Mount of Olives just two miles east of Jerusalem. Six days before the Passover ceremonies would begin (John 12:1), Jesus and His disciples arrived in the village of Bethany where Lazarus and his sisters lived. A banquet of food, some relaxation and close conversation with his dear friends provided much-needed restoration after the grueling trek through the Judean wilderness. Knowing as He did that His death was drawing nigh, this cherished time with friends must have been one filled with a sadness He couldn't express. Jesus had told His disciples that all of the predictions of the prophets would soon come true in Jerusalem and that He would be killed, but they did not understand what He meant. So many of His followers (including His disciples) still didn't realize why He had come to earth or who He really was. The sense of not being understood most likely cut into His heart, yet He continued on the course the Father had set before Him.

Jesus took the twelve aside and told them, "We are
going up to Jerusalem, and everything that is
written by the prophets about the Son of Man
will be fulfilled. He will be handed over to the
Gentiles. They will mock him, insult him, spit
on him, flog him and kill him. On the third
day he will rise again." The disciples did

> *not understand any of this. Its meaning was*
> *hidden from them, and they did not know*
> *what he was talking about.*

Luke 18:31-34, NIV

Jesus planned to spend Passover week in Bethany with friends, traveling the short distance to Jerusalem daily. After a night's rest and breakfast with His companions, Jesus arranged to go up to Jerusalem in preparation for the Passover. He told two of His disciples to go on ahead and return with a donkey they would find tethered along the way. This they did. They placed their cloaks upon the back of the animal and thus prepared the King of Kings to enter into the final week of His earthly life. Riding upon a donkey, a beast of burden, somehow did not fit with the scene of a triumphal king, yet this short ride along the olive tree-studded ridge known as the Mount of Olives, would be forever celebrated by believers.

> *Rejoice greatly, O Daughter of Zion! Shout, Daughter of*
> *Jerusalem! See, your king comes to you, righteous and*
> *having salvation, gentle and riding on a donkey,*
> *on a colt, the foal of a donkey.*

Zechariah 9:9, NIV

It is in this setting that we join the populace of Jerusalem. Throngs of people were in and around the city for the Passover and word quickly spread that Jesus was arriving. They scurried up and along the steep hillside of the ridge to get a glimpse of the Teacher, the Healer, the One who had brought Lazarus back from death. As He entered the area overlooking the city of Jerusalem, they cheered and shouted praises, spreading branches of palms (a symbol of the desire to be free at the time) on the stony dirt path before Him. They were ecstatic! The long-awaited One was here at last! Only days later, these same Passover celebrants would desert Him and shout, "CRUCIFY!"

Reaching the top of the mountain ridge, Jesus looked ahead, past the Garden of Gethsemane and across the Kidron Valley, toward the city. Tears of deepest sorrow and overwhelming sadness filled the eyes of the Creator as He looked down upon His beloved Jerusalem and as He spoke these heart-rending words, He began the slow descent into the valley toward the Eastern Gate.

As he approached Jerusalem and saw the city, he wept over
it and said, "If you, even you, had only known on this day
what would bring you peace—but now it is hidden from
your eyes. The days will come upon you when your
enemies will build an embankment against you
and encircle you and hem you in on every side.
They will dash you to the ground, you and
the children within your walls. They will
not leave one stone on another, because
you did not recognize the time of
God's coming to you."

Luke 19:41-44, NIV

Most would reject the one God had given them despite all the miracles they had seen. Once before, He had spoken words of God's love in a discussion with the Pharisees. His words have never been forgotten. They reach into the deepest recesses of our very being, where He resides. He is speaking to those who yet deny Him and He pleads in love.

O Jerusalem, Jerusalem, you who kill the prophets and
stone those sent to you, how often I have longed to
gather your children together, as a hen gathers
her chicks under her wings, but you were
not willing!

Luke 13:34, NIV

34. PRESENTATION OF THE LAMB

The LORD called to Moses and spoke to him from the Tent of Meeting. He said, "Speak to the Israelites and say to them: 'When any of you brings an offering to the LORD, bring as your offering an animal from either the herd or the flock. If the offering is a burnt offering from the herd, he is to offer a male without defect. He must present it at the entrance to the Tent of Meeting so that it will be acceptable to the LORD.'"

Leviticus 1:1-3, NIV

The prophet from Galilee was here and many people had rushed to greet and cheer Him during His descent from the Mount of Olives. Riding upon the donkey along the well-worn roadway, He passed the peaceful Garden of Gethsemane and entered the Kidron Valley before the procession headed uphill toward the Temple.

What was he thinking as He rode past the Gethsemane grove of olive trees? He already knew that in only a few days He would be pleading to the Father with such fervency that great drops of bloody sweat would ooze from His brow. He also knew He would be alone beneath the ancient trees, asking God if it were possible, could the physical and spiritual anguish of the following day be avoided.

He was human, after all—Jesus the man and Christ the Sacrifice—at the same time. He knew on that triumphal day that His chosen 12, who had lived and walked with Him for three years, would soon fail Him. These men, who had witnessed His power over all things, heard His teachings and observed His miracles, would each leave His side when He needed them most— one would even betray Him for a token amount of 30 pieces of silver, which according to Exodus 21:32 was the price of a slave.

Slowly the donkey plodded along the well-worn path that led to the Eastern Gate and from there to the Temple. Upon entering the gate, everything abruptly changed. The busyness and noise of the Temple area was stunning to the eyes and ears of any beholder, but especially to Jesus, whose Father resided there. The preparation for the Passover was but a cacophony, a marketplace of bleating, baying and cooing animals and birds waiting to be bought or sold for sacrifice and moneychangers at their designated tables, shouting above the din to make their voices heard. These flea market mercenaries were angrily driven away by Jesus. In fact, any who conducted business there were rebuked by Him for creating a bazaar of the Lord's Holy Temple.

During the time of the desert Tabernacle, the presentation of an animal to be sacrificed was always first brought before the priests in accordance with the very specific instructions given to Moses by God. [According to Leviticus 1:1-3 above, there is reason to believe that a thorough inspection was always performed. This would certainly infer that an inspection had to take place in order to determine that the animal was blemish free.]

This most triumphal day in Jerusalem over 2,000 years ago was in fact the very day when the people chose their spotless Passover lamb! God's timing is impeccable!

The priests, whose job it was to view and accept the sacrificial animals, either ignored or denied the Messiah. Those who were in a position to accept the perfect Lamb sacrifice reacted instead with anger and rebuttal, their vicious plans to trump up charges with which to arrest Him already festering in their evil minds. Amazingly, the Bible tells us that even some of these leaders believed in Him!

> *Yet at the same time many even among the leaders*
> *believed in him. But because of the Pharisees they*
> *would not confess their faith for fear they would*
> *be put out of the synagogue.*

John 12:42, NIV

The ultimate sacrifice, the Passover Lamb, pure and undefiled, was there among them, yet He was not acknowledged. No one recognized Him—no, not one, save His Father in Heaven.

He is still among us. Here is the Chosen One. See, He comes humbly on a donkey—the Savior of mankind. Do not pass Him by.

The next day John seeth Jesus coming unto him, and saith, "Behold the Lamb of God, which taketh away the sin of the world."

John 1:29, KJV

35. THE SEVEN FEASTS

The LORD said to Moses, "Speak to the Israelites and say to them: 'These are my appointed feasts, the appointed feasts of the LORD, which you are to proclaim as sacred assemblies.'"

Leviticus 23:1-2, NIV

Passover and the Feast of Unleavened Bread

Three times a year, the Lord required that all the men of Israel appear before Him for celebrations and after Solomon's Temple was built, Jerusalem was where He came to reside. Going up to Jerusalem during these specified feasts became a deep desire within the hearts of all those who wanted to obey and honor the Lord.

Three times a year all your men must appear before the LORD your God at the place he will choose: at the Feast of Unleavened Bread, the Feast of Weeks and the Feast of Tabernacles. No man should appear before the LORD empty-handed.

Deuteronomy 16:16, NIV

The first of these three festivals, the Feast of Unleavened Bread, coincided with the Passover. Beginning the day after the eve of Passover, this festival was to last seven days. God decreed that during this time, there could be no leavening in the homes of the Hebrews. Furthermore, He commanded that only unleavened bread would be eaten during those days in remembrance of God's deliverance of them from Egyptian slavery.

Feast of First Fruits

Following the onset of the Feast of Unleavened Bread, on the day after the Passover Sabbath, the Feast of First Fruits was celebrated. On this day, the Hebrews were to celebrate with joyous thanksgiving and praise to God the first grains of the harvest, knowing and believing that a full harvest was yet to come.

Feast of Weeks

*From the day after the Sabbath, the day you brought the
sheaf of the wave offering, count off seven full weeks.
Count off fifty days up to the day after the seventh
Sabbath, and then present an offering of new
grain to the LORD.*

Leviticus 23:15-16, NIV

Seven weeks after the Passover Sabbath, at the end of the barley harvest came the next celebration, one at which the grateful Hebrews thanked the Lord for the beginning of the wheat harvest. During this holiday, the priests offered two loaves of leavened bread to the Lord as a sampling of their yet-to-be-harvested wheat crops. "Shavuot," as this occasion is called in Hebrew means "weeks," but it was also known by its Greek name, Pentecost, which means 50.

Feast of Trumpets

After a period of months, the next feast to be observed was the Feast of Trumpets or Rosh Hashanah, a more solemn time of gathering together. The Hebrews were not to do any work on that day, but instead they were to worship God and offer a burnt sacrifice to Him. Heralded by the priests' loud blowing of trumpets (Leviticus 23:23-24), this feast was a call to worship for everyone.

God had told them at the time of the Tabernacle's raising to make two trumpets, one for signaling the people to assemble and one to break up the camp when it was time to move on. He further instructed them to use the trumpets when they went to war and also in times of gladness at their annual festivals (Numbers 10), with the promise that with the sound of the trumpets, He would come to their rescue and they would also be reminded of His covenant agreement with them.

This particular celebration grabbed my attention and prompted me to remember the importance of trumpet blasts regarding Joshua's astonishing conquest of Jericho as they entered the Promised Land. Regal and powerful is the sound of a trumpet!

> *Then the LORD said to Joshua, "See, I have delivered*
> *Jericho into your hands, along with its king and its*
> *fighting men. March around the city once with all*
> *the armed men. Do this for six days. Have seven*
> *priests carry trumpets of rams' horns in front*
> *of the ark. On the seventh day, march around*
> *the city seven times, with the priests blowing*
> *the trumpets. When you hear them sound a*
> *long blast on the trumpets, have all the*
> *people give a loud shout; then the wall*
> *of the city will collapse and*
> *the people will go up, every*
> *man straight in."*
>
> Joshua 6:2-5, NIV

Day of Atonement

This celebration, which is known as Yom Kippur, was held after the tenth day of the Festival of Weeks. This was the only day in the Hebrew calendar during which the high priest could enter the Holy of Holies beyond the curtain to beg forgiveness for the sins of himself and all Hebrews. At that time, he would bring the blood of a sacrificed animal as atonement for their sins.

> *For the life of the flesh is in the blood: and I have given it*
> *to you upon the altar to make an atonement for your*
> *souls: for it is the blood that maketh an*
> *atonement for the soul.*
>
> Leviticus 17:11, KJV

Feast of Booths

Perhaps the most jubilant of festivals was the Feast of Booths or Succoth, which was celebrated at the final fall harvest. The Hebrews were instructed by the Lord to gather tree branches and fall fruits with which to build tents as a reminder of the bountiful harvests provided by God. It is this autumn feast to which Gomar and his mother traveled in James Michener's previously mentioned book *The Source*. The tabernacles or booths, used as living quarters during the feast, punctuated the hillsides around Jerusalem with color and joy. It must have been an awesome and beautiful sight indeed!

As we enter into Jerusalem and the last week of Jesus' earthly life, perhaps you will see the hidden mysteries of the Old Testament Feasts and a connection with the purpose of Jesus' life and death. As you think about them, consider what they mean to you and what marvelous promises are yet to be fulfilled. Read more about the festivals and come to experience the joy that each one brought and still can bring to the life of a believer.

We have this hope as an anchor for the soul, firm and secure. It enters the inner sanctuary behind the curtain where Jesus, who went before us, has entered on our behalf. He has become a high priest forever in the order of Melchizedek.

Hebrews 6:19-20, NIV

36. MEMORIAM

...when I see the blood, I will pass over you.

Exodus 12:13, NIV

During the week, the Hebrews had been excitedly preparing for the annual commemoration of their deliverance from Egyptian slavery as instructed by God through Moses. The women brought out their finest dishes and thoroughly inspected their homes for any signs of leavened bread which had to be removed. The lamb was to be roasted, not boiled and eaten with bitter herbs which would serve to remind them of the bitterness of slavery. Because they left in such swiftness, there would not be time for kneading and allowing bread to rise. Thus, the eating of what represented the hastily-prepared exodus (unleavened bread) was also part of the remembrance.

In the time of Jesus, it was customary for each family to gather and as they leaned around a table, they shared the Passover meal. As they ate, the youngest child would ask questions about the celebration and the meal, just as God had directed. The father would then reply to each question in turn, explaining the meaning of the symbolic foods. In this way, the ancient tale of deliverance out of Egyptian slavery was repeated and preserved from generation to generation.

And in the future, your children will ask you, 'What does all this mean?' Then you will tell them, 'With the power of his mighty hand, the Lord brought us out of Egypt, the place of our slavery.'

Exodus 13:14, NLT

Jesus knew He was about to eat His last Passover with His earthly family, the ones who had spent three years with Him. He again reminded them that He would soon be killed.

During the meal, He also pointed out that it was Judas who would betray Him. Judas left at once, going out into the night (John 13:30, NLT).

> *When Jesus had finished saying all these things, he said to his disciples, "As you know, Passover begins in two days, and the Son of Man will be handed over to be crucified."*

Matthew 26:1-2, NLT

Even though He had told them only two days before that He would be betrayed and crucified (John 13:1), the disciples failed to comprehend that *He* was the true Passover sacrifice and that the shedding of His blood would provide everyone with deliverance from the bondage of sin forevermore. They did not know that He, God's perfect sacrifice from the beginning of time, was about to institute His own memorial.

In accordance with the ancient ritual, Jesus and His disciples shared the meal together remembering the blood of the lamb, the bitterness of slavery and the haste of preparation for the next morning's massive departure from Egypt. Think about that! The eating of the lamb (which required the shedding of innocent blood), the breaking of unleavened (sinless) bread (Jesus, the Bread of Life) and the bitter herbs of slavery (to sin)—all had been but symbols of His soon-to-be broken body and shed blood. There is much to consider when we read in the Bible the story of the last supper Jesus shared with His friends.

Take time to think about the meal and its symbolism regarding Jesus—we know He surely did. Consider His servant's heart which was displayed when He washed the feet of the twelve. Meditate on His awareness regarding the one He had known all along would betray Him. Pray with Him as you contemplate the acute knowledge He had that within hours, He would face arrest and suffer the inhumane torture of crucifixion. Most importantly, look within your heart and ponder the separation from God that He would soon endure as He hung upon the cross—your sins and mine upon Him. God, who cannot abide sin, would turn His face from His Son in this time of anguish in order to cover the cost of sin and because of that, when Jesus took His last breath, He would essentially die alone.

May we always remember the blood of Jesus, our Savior.

For you know that it was not with perishable things such as silver or gold that you were redeemed from the empty way of life handed down to you from your forefathers, but with the precious blood of Christ, a lamb without blemish or defect.

1 Peter 1:18-19, NIV

37. WHY THIS NIGHT?

*In days to come, when your son asks you, 'What
does this mean?' say to him, 'With a mighty
hand the LORD brought us out of Egypt,
out of the land of slavery.'*

Exodus 13:14, NIV

When the evening meal concluded, Jesus and the
remaining 11 disciples sang a hymn from one of the Psalms
for this was a traditional closure for the Passover meal. They
then walked through the city toward the Garden of
Gethsemane, a place where they often met to talk or pray.
Upon their arrival, Jesus told His closest friends that each
one of them would desert Him that very night. They listened
incredulously, denying such a thing could ever happen, but
it did—just as He said.

Then all the disciples deserted him and fled.

Matthew 26:56, NIV

Knowing the time of His betrayal and arrest was near,
Jesus walked a short distance away in order to be alone and
pray, asking them to wait for Him to return. Twice He came
back to check on His friends and both times they had fallen
asleep. Suddenly, the quiet setting was disrupted by a
shouting pack of malevolent men who were armed with
swords and clubs. Judas approached and greeted Jesus with
a kiss and with this treacherous act, his lips presented the
rejected Lamb of God to the servants of the high priests.

What followed was a travesty of justice as Jesus was
brutally led from one location to another. Throughout the

long night, a total of six trials were conducted by both Jewish and Roman authorities. They tried to trump up evidence against Him and were unsuccessful; Jesus, the gentle prophet from Galilee, was sentenced to death without ever being formally charged with a crime. Toward morning, an exhausted Jesus, battered and bleeding from the scourging ordered by Herod, was brought before Pilate a second time. Although Pilate could find no fault with Him and desired His release, he allowed the commanding crowd to decide Jesus' fate rather than risk a Passover riot. Given the choice, many of the very people who had cheered for Him only days before eagerly demanded Jesus' crucifixion rather than condemn the murderer Barabbas.

Jesus' final steps would lead Him to the place outside the city limits known as "The Skull." Weakened by blood loss from the scourging and crown of long thorns forced upon His head by the laughing Roman soldiers, He was made to carry His own cross (John 19:17). It wasn't long, however, before a man named Simon of Cyrene, who just happened to be coming into the city, was forced to follow and carry Jesus' cross as this ghastly parade of sorrow moved its way through the narrow streets of the city of God.

Jesus was crucified at nine o'clock in the morning. His cross was placed between those of two others who had been sentenced to the same fate. The Romans favored this brutal form of execution, for it was one which allowed for long-suffering of the victim while providing a beastly warning to anyone who would dare to defy them.

Hanging there between two men who had committed the crime of murder, the innocent Lamb of God was able to offer eternal life once more before His earthly ministry came to a close. One, a scoffer, derided Jesus, daring Him to save all three of them if He was indeed the Messiah. The other acknowledged his own sin and asked Jesus to remember him when He entered His Kingdom. Jesus assured the repentant one that He would with this promise:

> *Jesus answered him, "I tell you the truth,*
> *today you will be with me in paradise."*

Luke 23:43, NIV

By noon, the light from the sun was gone and utter darkness pervaded the whole land for three hours. At the same time, the curtain in the Temple that separated man from the Holy of Holies was torn in half.

It was now about the sixth hour, and darkness came over the whole land until the ninth hour, for the sun stopped shining. And the curtain of the temple was torn in two.

Luke 23:44-45, NIV

At about three o'clock, the moribund Jesus shouted out to God saying,

"...My God, my God, why have you forsaken me?"

Matthew 27:46, NIV

There was no voice from Heaven. The weight of the sins of all mankind had been placed upon Him—the price had been paid. God the Father had turned His face from His beloved Son who sinned not and yet bore all sin. Jesus cried out once more before He released His spirit and died, leaving His spilled blood beneath the cross.

Why is this night different from any other? I believe a quote from Paul, a slave of Jesus Christ, will provide a more than satisfactory answer:

I have discovered this principle of life—that when I want to do what is right, I inevitably do what is wrong. I love God's law with all my heart. But there is another power within me that is at war with my mind. This power makes me a slave to the sin that is still within me. Oh, what a miserable person I am! Who will free me from this life that is dominated by sin and death? Thank God! The answer is in Jesus Christ our Lord. So you see how it is: In my mind I really want to obey God's law, but because of my sinful nature I am a slave to sin.

Romans 7:21-25, NLT

We no longer need to remain slaves to sin and our own sinful nature. We can become free at last because of what Jesus did for us. This long Passover night was for you and me, my friend. Jesus only asks that you accept His undying love. He welcomes you to come under the protection of His sinless blood, for with your willingness to trust Him with all that you are, your exodus will begin.

> *But if we walk in the light, as he is in the light, we have fellowship with one another, and the blood of Jesus, his Son, purifies us from all sin.*

1 John 1:7, NIV

38. GOLGOTHA

We all, like sheep, have gone astray, each of us has
turned to his own way; and the LORD has laid
on him the iniquity of us all.

Isaiah 53:6, NIV

Through pools of tears that clouded her sight, Mary looked down at the blood-soaked, muddy earth beneath the cross. Her clothing, long since saturated with the crimson blood of her precious son, now was a matted, sodden mixture of the hideous hues of death...blood no longer red, but instead dark, almost black, grotesquely congealed and mixed with dirt, stones and tears.

How long she had been on her knees was of no consequence. Exhausted from weeping and bereft of solace, she finally lay down in the shadow of her beloved son's mutilated body, void of tears for the moment and empty of spirit forever it seemed.

"How could it be? This can't be true—everything within me denies the reality of this unspeakable day."

"He is my son," she sobbed to her Father in Heaven. "I cannot bear this pain. How can a mother still be alive when the fruit of her womb has suffered the horrors of this day? I would have given my life for His," she cried in anguish. "My blood for His. I pray it could have been so, even though I know, Father, that you said long ago He would be taken from us in such a way." Mary knew at that moment she was living the prophecy made by old Simeon outside the Temple after he had blessed them..."a sword will pierce even your own soul" (Luke 2:35, NASB).

"I am blessed that You chose me to give birth to Him, to raise Him as a little baby to childhood and on to manhood. What a precious child He was—so filled with unconditional love for everyone who came in contact with Him—so respectful—so generous—and such a help to His father Joseph and me! The sparkle in His eyes brought such light to all of us—to everyone He knew."

God, in His matchless way, provided comfort to the deeply grieving mother. From somewhere close by, she heard soft sounds of sobbing and praying as others suffered their deep sense of disbelief and hopelessness. She was in her own world of pain and barely aware of them, yet the sounds reminded her she was not alone. From somewhere in the misty space in which Mary lay, a presence attended to her and lifted her quivering body from the ground. The strong arms of John enfolded her body and with it, her weakness. Hot, wet tears coursed down the crooked creases of his rugged, bearded face and mixed with the grimy, dried tears he had shed, creating a tapestry of unbelievable sorrow. Together they looked upon the body of Jesus their Savior as it was tenderly lowered to the ground.

Again she gazed upward, this time beyond the empty space on the cruel and bitter tree upon which His body had been impaled, beyond the malevolent black clouds the empty cross now pierced, onward toward Heaven. Mary pleaded silently, "Oh, help me, Lord, to accept this day as what You have chosen it to be—a day of torture and suffering, a day that seems hopeless and bleak, a day of Your choosing—let me remember it is a day that will bring salvation to the world. I do not understand, but yet I *believe* that my Son has become the LIGHT of the world on this, the darkest day of my life. Please help me to accept Your will as my own."

Then Mary said, "Behold the maidservant of the Lord! Let it be to me according to your word."

Luke 1:38, NKJV

39. AN EMPTY TOMB

*He had done no wrong and had never deceived
anyone. But he was buried like a criminal;
he was put in a rich man's grave.*

Isaiah 53:9, NLT

When the Sabbath was over, some of the women purchased embalming spices, planning to return in the morning to the new rock-hewn tomb belonging to Joseph of Arimathea, where Jesus' body had been laid to rest.

*At the place where Jesus was crucified, there was a
garden, and in the garden a new tomb, in which
no one had ever been laid.*

John 19:41, NIV

When they arrived, there was a great earthquake, for an angel of the Lord came down from Heaven, rolled the stone away and sat upon it! The angel explained that Jesus had risen and told the women to go quickly and tell His disciples that Jesus was going to Galilee to meet them there. As they ran from the tomb, they came across Jesus Himself. A mixture of feelings—joy, fear, anxiety, disbelief—assaulted their senses.

The last time they had seen His body, it had been disfigured beyond recognition due to the unspeakable torture to which it had been subjected. Now, here in the same garden, close to where they had placed Him in the tomb, appeared Jesus in His resurrected body, made new and undefiled! It was quite incomprehensible to these ones who, although they believed Jesus was the Messiah, nevertheless did not really expect Him to return from death!

Over the days that followed, word quickly spread around the city that the crucified prophet from Galilee, supposedly dead since Friday, was no longer in the tomb. Wild stories began to fly, many of which were frequently embellished by gossips and people who wanted to speculate just to hear themselves talk. Occasionally, even long-time skeptics were wondering if it could possibly be true, when some among His friends boldly insisted He had returned from death.

At the gates where men met to discuss things, the incredible occurrence was disputed.

"Impossible!"

"Arisen from the dead? Of *course* not risen from the dead!"

"Who could believe such a thing? His friends probably stole His body, that's what!"

"No! I think the priests stole it! Remember...He said He would arise after three days. They would want to make sure *that* didn't happen!"

"Yes, that's true enough, but on the other hand, if *the priests* stole it, they would be *bragging* about it, telling *everyone* He didn't come back from death! They would be announcing it and inviting everyone to come and observe saying, 'See? Here is His body in this second tomb, right where we placed it!'"

The Roman soldiers had other thoughts and suspicions about the so-called "resurrection" of Jesus.

"Ha! Those brave Temple police guarded the tomb of the crucified man, did they? I have it on trusted authority that they got so frightened out there that they all fainted!"

"Yes and when they woke up, they ran all the way to the Temple to tell the priests about their 'ghostly' experience at the tomb...such fearless, valiant soldiers! Cowards—all of them!"

"Well, the story I heard—and I have good resources from some who work at the Temple—is that those Temple leaders who had hired them got together and bribed the guards. 'Just tell everyone you fell asleep, they were told. We'll back you up if anyone asks.'"

*When the chief priests had met with the elders and devised
a plan, they gave the soldiers a large sum of money, telling
them, "You are to say, 'His disciples came during the
night and stole him away while we were asleep.'"*

Matthew 28:12-13, NIV

Elsewhere in the city, solicitous women, meeting at the well, the grinding place or in front of their homes, had other thoughts about the "miracle."

"Who knows? He was weak from bleeding! The poor man didn't have a drop of water to drink all day! We've all seen how merciless those soldiers are—they do this just for sport, you know! Taking bets and gambling for their clothes—they have no pity on the criminals! Why, I..."

"No! I disagree with you! I think the women just went to the wrong tomb; they were all in such a hurry to bury Him because Sabbath was about to start and it was getting dark. I'm sure they forgot where He was buri..."

Another woman interrupted. "But the blood—it was *every-where*...all over Him and buckets of it on the ground beneath the cross—maybe even *all* His blood! I heard that when He died and the soldier stabbed Him in His side, nothing came out but some blood and water! That spells 'dead' to me! There is no way He could have lived and even if He had, how could He have moved that massive stone they rolled in front of the tomb?"

"The blood...What did it mean?" asked one young girl who had been standing alone near the well listening to the discussion. "I was there too, and someone in the crowd said He was the Lamb of God. It was Passover and lambs were being sacrificed at the Temple at the same time. Do you think it means something? I even heard one of the Roman soldiers say this: 'Truly, He was the Son of God!'"

The women ignored her.

She sobbed and whispered, as if to herself, "What if He *was* the Son of God? Just what if He *was*?" She stumbled away, head lowered, shoulders trembling and tears blurring her vision. She walked endlessly throughout the city that day, repeating to no one in particular, "What if He *was*? What can I *do*?"

To this day, there remains the age-old stir regarding Jesus' resurrection. We who believe know that we don't have to wander the lonely streets of our lives, endlessly asking what we can do about Him. Jesus did not leave us alone to wander hopelessly searching for answers. We can look beyond the hype, the questions and the rumors because the true story isn't to be found among the words of rumormongers, in storybooks, theoretical tomes or biographies. The story of Jesus is found in the Bible.

Jesus has *always* been—and *forever* will be the Savior! The Bible is His true biography and it begins in Genesis, the first book of the Bible. He is present in all 66 books, hidden at first in the Old Testament and then made gloriously manifest in the New Testament.

> *"God in His weakness—Christ dying on the cross—*
> *is far stronger than any man."*
>
> 1 Corinthians 1:25, TLB

What shall you do?

Each one of us still must decide to either believe this wonderful Good News or close our minds and refuse to accept it—the choice is still ours. Read and believe in God's Word and pray for understanding as you study the Bible. Believe in the power of His love and believe in His resurrection. As you lean on these truths, God will guide your life and reveal such wonders to you that your mind cannot contain it all. It is written for you. Just believe!

> *But God raised Him from the dead, and for many days He*
> *was seen by those who had traveled with Him from*
> *Galilee to Jerusalem. They are now His witnesses*
> *to our people.*
>
> Acts 13:30-31, NIV

40. ABIDING GIFT

This is the word of the LORD to Zerubbabel: 'Not by might nor by power, but by my Spirit,' says the LORD Almighty.

Zechariah 4:6, NIV

What would it take to turn the world upside down?

Devout followers who denied the truth despite everything they had been taught and had witnessed?

Cowering, fearful men hiding behind locked doors?

Doubters who saw a man brought back from the grave, yet who nevertheless disbelieved Jesus could also return from death?

Such were the disciples of Jesus, the very ones who over the three years of His earthly ministry consistently saw, heard and experienced His incredible power over all things. They were sad replicas of what they once had been, yet something astounding was soon to occur, something which would transform them from trembling, frightened weaklings into bold men of authority who would affect the world forever. It happened in the short span of just ten days.

It takes so much more than the weakness of ordinary men to change the world—it takes power, authority, conviction and commitment—all attributes uncommon to Jesus' disciples during the days of His trial, crucifixion and even after He had arisen.

They loved Him, were devoted to Him and were lost and bereft of hope when He died—of that we read in the gospels. Nevertheless, Jesus planned to use these pathetic men, regardless of their character flaws, because He knew that after He returned to the Father, a greater power would come upon them. They *would* be changed, they *would* be empowered, and they *would* tell the world about the Kingdom of Heaven!

After appearing to the disciples numerous times following His resurrection, Jesus again explained that He must leave them and return to His Father. He promised that He would ask the Father to send One who would comfort, teach and embolden them to share this Good News with the entire world. Furthermore, the Comforter would help them as they witnessed by bringing to their minds all that He had told them.

Jesus understood their fear, but brought them peace, not condemnation or accusations.

On the evening of that first day of the week, when the disciples were together, with the doors locked for fear of the Jews, Jesus came and stood among them and said, "Peace be with you!"

John 20:19-20, NIV

In spite of this visit, eight days later they were still meeting secretly, in fear and apprehension. Later, He met with them in Galilee while they were out on the lake fishing. He called out to them from the shore and advised them where to find a great catch of fish. When they brought the boat in, He had prepared a fire and even cooked breakfast for them, somewhat reminiscent of their days together.

For 40 days, He appeared in His resurrected form not only to them, but to many others as well, before His ascension to Heaven from the Mount of Olives. Since this area overlooked the city of Jerusalem and the Temple, it might be that this amazing, perhaps even frightening sight was visible to the residents of the city and even to the priests serving at the Temple.

Each and every prophecy of the Scriptures regarding Jesus was to be fulfilled and as He rose from the earth into a cloud, two angels appeared to reassure the observers that Jesus indeed would return.

They were looking intently up into the sky as he was going, when suddenly two men dressed in white stood beside them. "Men of Galilee," they said, "why do you stand here looking into the sky? This same Jesus, who has

164

been taken from you into heaven, will come back in the same way you have seen him go into heaven."

Acts 1:10-11, NIV

There are prophecies in the Word of God yet to be fulfilled. One is concerning His return, for which all believers eagerly yearn.

On that day his feet will stand on the Mount of Olives, east of Jerusalem, and the Mount of Olives will be split in two from east to west, forming a great valley, with half of the mountain moving north and half moving south.

Zechariah 14:4, NIV

A transformation began that day in the minds and spirits of the disciples. After Jesus ascended, they left the Mount of Olives, walked back to Jerusalem and held a prayer meeting which lasted several days. Peter announced during this time that they needed someone to replace Judas and that it must be someone who had been with them continually from the day of Jesus' baptism until the present (Acts 1:21-22). It was only after much prayer that Mathias was chosen as the twelfth apostle.

Jesus had told the disciples to remain in Jerusalem until they received the gift He had asked for, the gift which God was going to send them. Did they really comprehend what the gift was? Did they understand about the ability to witness to the world with the strength of true conviction? Did they realize that the enabling power and confidence which was to come upon them was real and not just a superstitious fairy tale? Even after seeing Jesus as He ascended into the clouds, could they have ever comprehended what was about to occur just ten days later?

When the day of Pentecost came, they were all together in one place. Suddenly a sound like the blowing of a violent wind came from heaven and filled the whole house where they were sitting. They saw what seemed to be tongues of fire that separated and came to rest on each of them. All of them were filled with the Holy Spirit and began to speak in other tongues as the Spirit enabled them.

Acts 2:1-4, NIV

From that day forward, these men were never the same. Buoyed with the power of the Holy Spirit, they faithfully proclaimed Jesus and the Kingdom of God for the rest of their lives, eventually giving their lives as martyrs for His sake. Yet, it was not by their power nor by their might, but by the power of the indwelling of the Holy Spirit who came and dwelt within them that day, that they were able to continue the course set before them by their Savior.

What did it take to turn the world upside down? It took ordinary men filled with the power of the Holy Spirit to do Jesus' bidding. They *did* change the world and it has never been the same. We— you and I—can go and do likewise.

> *But you will receive power when the Holy Spirit comes on you; and you will be my witnesses in Jerusalem, and in all Judea and Samaria, and to the ends of the earth.*

Acts 1:8, NIV

While we are still in Jerusalem, about to conclude this journey through the Holy Land, may I beseech you to ask the Lord to renew your strength, your faith and your commitment? He is able and willing to give you all that you need to serve Him according to His wonderful plan for your life. When fear, anxiety and doubt plague you, remember He is the God who keeps all promises. He will bring you through any difficulty if you determine in your heart to follow the Lamb.

If you have never accepted His free gift of eternal life, you can do so now. Say a prayer to God, acknowledge His Son Jesus as the Lord of your life. Welcome Him into your heart and He will come and abide with you forever. Please don't leave Jerusalem without your gift.

> *If ye love me, keep my commandments. And I will pray the Father, and he shall give you another Comforter, that he may abide with you for ever.*

John 14:15-16, KJV

*Jesus did many other things as well. If every one of
them were written down, I suppose
that even the whole world would not
have room for the books that
would be written.*

John 21:25, NIV

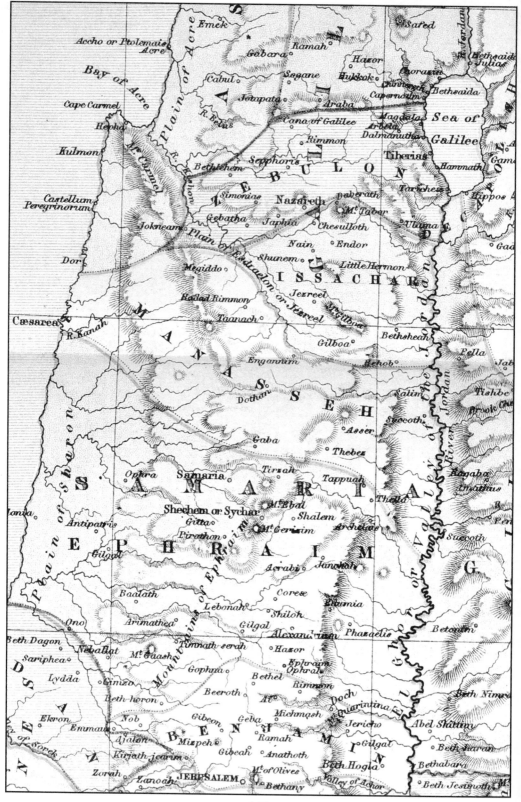

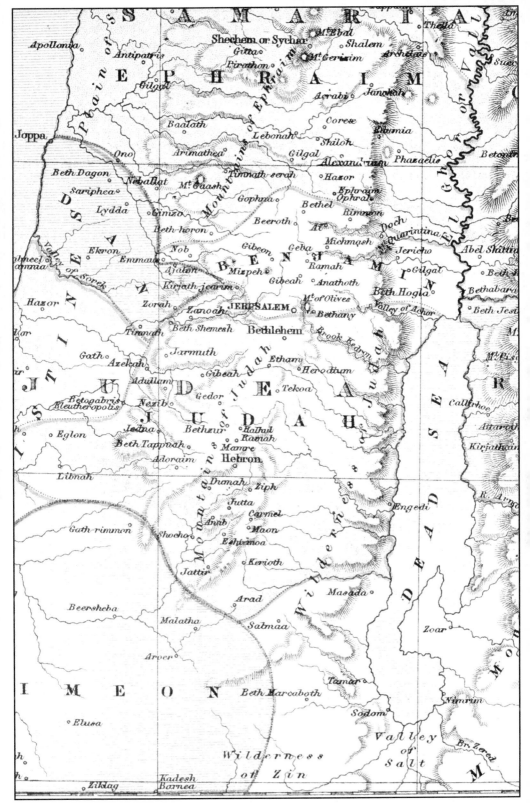

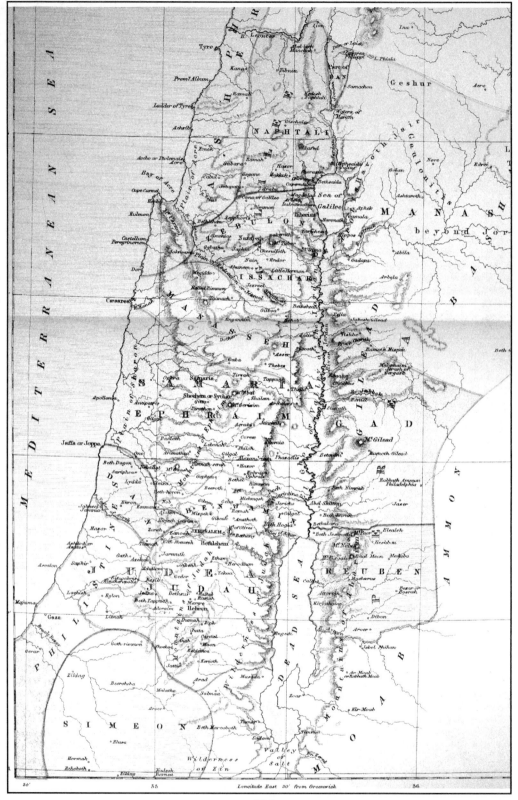